A COW NEEDS A TAIL FOR MORE THAN ONE SUMMER

LIFE LESSONS FROM MOM

by Lolita Cummings Carson

A Cow Needs A Tail For More Than One Summer
Copyright © 2015 Lolita Cummings Carson

Published by:
Blooming Twig Books
320 S. Boston, Suite 1026
Tulsa, OK 74103
www.bloomingtwig.com

All rights reserved. This book may not be photocopied for personal or professional use. No part of this book may be reproduced, stored in a retrieval system, or transmitted in any form or by any means (electronic, mechanical, photocopying, recording, or otherwise) without permission in writing from the author or publisher.

Hardcover: 978-1-61343-108-5
Paperback: 978-1-61343-107-8
Ebook: 978-1-61343-106-1

First Edition

Printed in the United States of America.

A COW NEEDS A TAIL FOR MORE THAN ONE SUMMER

LIFE LESSONS FROM MOM

by Lolita Cummings Carson

DEDICATION

For Mom and Dad—Mildred L. and the late Charles William Cummings—the most supportive, encouraging, loving, generous, and protective parents ever.

Charles William and Mildred L. Cummings

TABLE OF CONTENTS

Introduction	1
A fool and his money will soon be parted	5
If brains was dynamite, you couldn't blow your nose	11
If I tell you a hen dips snuff, you look under the wing	15
It's your little red wagon—you can push it or pull it	27
Laziness will kill you	33
I've already fallen out of that tree you're trying to climb	37
Check the oil, not the gas, 'cause some things will take care of themselves	47
It's gonna be teddy and the bear—and the old bear's gonna be on top	57
A cow needs a tail for more than one summer	67
Pride comes before the fall	75
Final thoughts	81
Tell us your story…	83
Acknowledgements	85
Testimonials	87
About the Author	89

= = = = = =
INTRODUCTION

I'll start with a confession: I'm as surprised as anyone that this book has been mass produced. Written? Yes, that was my plan. But available for all to see? Now, there's the shocker.

I wrote the first story for this book some years ago to honor my mother, Mildred L. Cummings. I did so shortly after losing my father, the late Charles William Cummings, to Alzheimer's, and it occurred to me that documenting these stories would be a perfect way to honor my mother while she was still alive.

As is Alzheimer's way, my father was slowly taken away in a hateful manner, one that afforded me the time to tell him I loved him, something he had heard over and over again during our lives. But, through the processes of denial, paralyzing fear, anger, and despair, I never really got into the nitty-gritty details and examples of why I loved him so. That didn't come until his funeral. He heard it in heaven, but he should have enjoyed it on earth.

It took a while, but, once grief began to loosen its grip, I promised not to make the same mistake twice. My mother would not just know that I love her, but she would know intimately why I love her.

My plan was to write a story or two, take them to a local printer for pretty, but inexpensive binding, and present them to Mom on her next birthday or Mother's Day.

Yep, that was the plan. Along the way, however, I asked for the opinions of various people—and they loved the stories. So much so, in fact, that they encouraged me to keep writing and to share the stories with audiences wider than my immediate family and circle of friends. Eventually, they actually persuaded me to write this book.

So what's it all about? Mom and her hilarious sayings.

Mom and Dad hailed from the deepest, most country part of Mississippi possi-

Big Mama's House in Mantachie, MS
Photo courtesy of Betty Cummings

ble—Mantachie. She loved it, but it was a rural area that a Michigan-reared "city girl" like me hated to no end. I was still forced to visit every summer as a child.

It was while she was growing up in Mantachie that my mother heard the peculiar sayings you will read in this book. Most came from her own mother, and were passed along to me and my sisters. Now, I just said "passed along" as if they were some great treasure, and I suppose they probably are now. But they sure didn't feel like it when I heard them repeatedly while growing up.

The first time I heard many of these sayings, my response was similar to the responses of Jesus' disciples when he told them parables. A quizzical look on my face, I'm sure, revealed that I had no idea what my mother was talking about. But, never the shy one, Mom was always willing to break down the words and interpret the meanings for me. To be honest, most times I didn't particularly like the lesson, but I had to admit the applicability and truthfulness of it—even if only to myself.

Yet now that I'm all grown up with adult children of my own, I really do cherish the wisdom and humor in these sayings—not just as they relate to child-rearing, but also in everyday life.

It has become increasingly clear that the application of these sayings extends far beyond reeling in a defiant child like me. In the process of my writing, these quirky sayings brought to mind lessons about personal and corporate responsibility, financial literacy, health management, hard work, choices, consequences, honesty, trust, and simply doing what's right. As luck would have it, these are all areas in which I have a great deal of expertise and an abundance to say.

INTRODUCTION

In any event, it's only fitting that I share these sayings with you. Maybe you've heard some, but not others. Maybe you'll pass them on to your children or grandchildren—or start to use them in your everyday life. Maybe you'll just read a bit about my never-one-for-the-easy-road childhood shenanigans and thank God your child is more obedient. I don't know. But regardless of your final action, I just hope you enjoy yourself while flipping through these pages. Life is too short for anything less.

Many Blessings!

Lolita

A FOOL AND HIS MONEY WILL SOON BE PARTED

Repetition. My mother loved it.

When I was a child, I was certain it had something to do with her admiration of the sound of her own voice. She seemingly never tired of it, but all I heard was the sound of a scratched vinyl record with the silver needle stuck in the same groove of the black disc, spinning her annoying voice to the same screeching lyrics over and over and over again.

Lita do this. Lita do that. Lita, Lita, Lita…. But now that I've graduated to being a parent, let's just say I'm singing a slightly similar tune myself. (Funny how that happens.)

In any event, I was quite the independent little sprite while growing up. I wanted, no, I needed, my own stuff. My own stash of chocolate and Sweet Tarts, my own brightly colored cotton tops and ratty blue jeans (no girly dresses required), my own yellow-paged Amelia Bedelia chapter books, and, yes, my own green-as-it came money. I wouldn't characterize myself as selfish, but there is something about sole ownership that still beckons me today.

It didn't necessarily matter to me how much money I had, as long as it afforded me the finer things in life—milk chocolate and other enticing sugar goodies that sustained my eighty-pound skinny-legged frame.

But it did matter to me a great deal that I maintained complete control over what jingled in my lint and candy-infested pocket. And therein laid the rub. My mother was a real skinflint. She'd squeeze a nickel until the buffalo screamed, so she didn't always take a liking to how I spent my money.

"Frivolous," she'd say. "Foolish," she'd mutter. "Careless." All I could hear, though, was yada, yada, yada, grumble, grumble, grumble. There's that record again.

At the time, I was sure she was overstepping her boundary on the money issue. My thought was that if I worked hard enough to put a dollar into my little paw, who was she to tell me how to spend it? Since the amount in question was pretty miniscule and not in danger of bankrupting any small nations, most times she'd back off and let me buy what was dancing in my eye.

But to my dismay, she never conceded before walking away, shaking her head from side-to-side with an annoying and smug expression overtaking her smooth brown face, mumbling what seemed to me one of her favorite, worn-out phrases—a fool and his money will soon be parted.

Most times I simply disregarded her mutterings on the subject with equal haughtiness. After all, if I earned the money, didn't I have every right to spend it as I saw fit?

She hadn't helped me work like a slave while cleaning my neighbor's house. No, that was I, and I alone, with so much sweat dripping into my burning eyes that I was convinced I'd someday need a leader dog. I also couldn't remember my mom helping me pick black-eyed peas and tomatoes in the garden while the pesky mosquitoes had their vampire-like way with my tender little arms and legs. No, that was all me.

My hustle, my money.

So, if I earned the money all alone, shouldn't I be able to spend it all alone?

I seemed to remember that basic lesson from one of my favorite childhood books, The Little Red Hen. Wasn't that the whole point of ownership?

Yep, I justified that one well enough so that I never gave my mother's prophesies a second thought—that was until the infamous "penny affair," as it later came to be known.

As a ten-year-old, I normally avoided shopping at all costs. Most trips seemed like an endless, torture-filled journey. We stopped at far too many stores for my taste. As soon as we stepped in, the strong scent of new fabric, especially ruffles and lace, repelled me. I knew my mother's next request would be for me to twirl around in one of those prissy little dresses.

A FOOL AND HIS MONEY WILL SOON BE PARTED

Now for some girls, that would have been an afternoon delight, looking like a Southern Belle ready for the next big ball. But for me, it was a trip to the shadowy depths of Hades—pure hell. For one, I was a tomboy. So, in my mind, I needed a new dress like I needed a sugarless diet. There was nothing desirable about it.

Secondly, while we were out shopping for worthless clothes, I was missing some of the best kick-ball games ever played. And, of course, I was the "star" player. Everyone wanted me on their team. I did for kickball what Babe Ruth did for baseball. I could swagger up to the plate, point far into the outfield, and send that ball sailing straight to the desired destination—or further. I owned that game!

But, finally, and most importantly, I HATED ruffles and lace.

Forty years later, it still makes me itch thinking about it. Whoever invented those frills had absolutely no regard for comfort—or little girls. I can't recall how many Saturdays I cried myself to sleep just thinking about what I'd have to wear to church the following day. Then on Sunday, I'd squirm, shuffle, and whine so much in those dresses that I never quite paid attention to the week's sermon. God himself, in all His glowing splendor, could have walked past my pew, and I would have missed the whole thing.

To this day, Mom still says I put on quite a show, like a little worm in hot ashes.

By the time we returned home, most of the skin on the back of my neck would have abandoned my body and attached itself to the mean-spirited ruffles that lined my collar. Even today, I don't own a single piece of clothing that itches or scratches.

No ruffles. No lace. Just one hundred percent soft cotton and other comfy fabrics. That's all a girl really needs.

So, whenever I knew my mom had a shopping trip planned, I avoided her like the plague. If I heard her come up the stairs, I'd hide deep in my closet behind all of the clothes she was constantly reminding me to put on hangers.

If she called for me while I was outside, I'd hide behind the nearest object that was bigger than me, and later deny I was within earshot of her voice.

Yes, avoidance was a sneaky tactic I used well, that is, unless her destination was Meijer Thrifty Acres, our local superstore. And why wouldn't I?

They had everything! Candy, toys, bikes, donuts, cotton candy, games. They even had Sandy, a mechanical pony kids could ride for a penny, and more gumball machines than any other store in the whole wide world. Yep, Meijer Thrifty Acres was a kid's heaven!

Normally when we shopped at Meijer, the colorful bags of cotton candy attracted my attention more than anything else. For less than a single dollar, they somehow managed to pack four different colors and flavors of the sweet, sticky confection into a humongous plastic bag and send you on your way happy as a clam.

But on this particular day, a dollar was about fifty cents right of my budget, so I shifted my attention to the gumball machines. Not exactly cotton candy, but enough to add a skip to my step as I headed in that direction.

Then something magical happened. I was making a mission-driven beeline for the machine with the brightly colored fist-sized gumballs when, all of a sudden, my attention was diverted to a machine holding nothing but copper pennies.

How could this be? Everyone, including me, knew I was the world's most hopeless sugar-fiend, yet here I was heading in the direction of a boring bronze metal machine? Something was surely amiss here.

But when I got closer, I realized why I had been so quickly sidetracked. These were no ordinary pennies. Oh, nooooo. These were rare, limited-edition pennies, and I knew immediately I was one lucky girl to have a shot at actually owning one of those little babies.

Soon, I became conscious of the fact I was in the presence of something "spectacular" indeed. Instead of the penny containing just one head, that of Abraham Lincoln, I was standing within spitting distance of a two-headed penny, one that

Lolita's pride and glory–if only for a moment.

contained the face of one of my favorite presidents, John F. Kennedy, along with Abraham Lincoln.

How lucky was I? Was this a joke? Was I on Candid Camera, or did I just have a horseshoe stuck up my rear?

A FOOL AND HIS MONEY WILL SOON BE PARTED

At that point, I decided to be quick and decisive. There was no time to tarry. So before anyone could say, "jackrabbit," I slid my quarter into the machine's narrow silver slot, turned the cold metal knob, and was soon thereafter in total awe as I held my very own two-headed penny.

It was all quite exciting. I could feel my heart thumping two beats for every one and prickles traveling over my entire body. I even broke out into a small sweat—that is until my mom came along.

When I stuck out my prepubescent chest and proudly revealed my major find, she looked at the penny, and then she looked at me. I found it hard to decipher the quizzical look on her face, so I studied her more while she studied me, wrinkled her brow, looked at the penny, and then moved toward the twenty-five cent sign on the machine. Finally, she spoke.

"Do you know what you've done, Lita?" she asked slowly and with an annoyed hesitation in her voice.

"Sure," I beamed. "I just purchased a special two-headed penny. Isn't it cool?"

"No, Lita," she said. "It's not cool. It's a rip-off. And you just got ripped. You just gave this machine a quarter, knowing full well you were going to get a penny in return. Did you think about that?"

"Well, of course I thought about that," I said with all the confidence I could muster.

Actually, I had not. There simply was no time to think when I saw the deal of the century flash right before my eyes.

"But it's no ordinary penny," I countered. "It's a special two-headed penny."

"Well, tell me," she said. "How much penny candy do you think you're going to be able to buy with your 'special' two-headed penny the next time you go to the store?"

And then it hit me. Jiminy Crickets—I'd been had! The stunned look on my face was exactly what she had hoped she'd see. I could see the smug satisfaction in her eyes.

And then she just had to say it while slowing walking away.... "A fool and his money will soon be parted."

A FOOL AND HIS MONEY WILL SOON BE PARTED

= = = = = =
IF BRAINS WAS DYNAMITE, YOU COULDN'T BLOW YOUR NOSE

Let's face it. Kids are prone to do some pretty stupid stuff.

Dad let a lot of crap just slide by. He understood the folly of youth and had, as Mom put it, the patience of Job. Only the most extreme acts of lunacy got under his skin.

Mom, on the other hand, marched around regularly with a dangerously short fuse that was ignited at the first sign of idiocy. In our house, it was a near-constant state that would elicit her usual standard first response.

"Really, Lita?" Mom would ask. "That's what you're doing? That's got to be one of the dumbest things I've ever seen you do. I'll tell you, if brains was dynamite, you couldn't blow your nose."

Normally my older sister, Jean, was compliant. When Mom and Dad told her to jump, she'd simply ask how high. Given the same command, I'd first want to know why, then when, where, on which foot, how far, for how long, what sense it made, who else was doing it, and when I finally had them against the ropes, I'd circle back to why. Jean was far too compliant.

Most of the time, Jean and I were polar opposites. But that all ceased on a bright sunny day in mid-June 1974. Jean was fourteen and had watched me get away with bloody murder long enough to give in to a little rebellion of her own. She'd gotten a new umbrella days before and was still enthralled by its novelty. At ten, I was curious about her fascination with something as elementary as an umbrella, but, as usual, didn't give it much thought before going about my business.

It was a nice umbrella—the fancy bubble-type with a non-assuming clear plastic dome on top and a steel four-inch pointy base that doubled as a walking stick on bottom. Yep, that little baby screamed reliability.

THE STEEP PRICE FOR SATURDAY MORNING BREAKFAST

Jean had been fiddling with her umbrella for only a few minutes before mom told her to put it away and prepare for our Saturday morning ritual. Mom spent most Saturday mornings cleaning the house and expected everyone else to join in the "fun." She'd begin making her rounds to our bedrooms as early as 8:00 a.m., telling us what a beautiful day it was and that it was time to get up and enjoy it.

For Mom, "enjoying the day" meant starting with a hearty breakfast that often consisted of sausage, scrambled eggs, country ham, grits, oatmeal, and homemade biscuits, and then cleaning the house from top to bottom.

That was Mom's idea of a good start Saturday. Mine went something like this: sleep until noon or so, catch whatever breakfast was left (hoping for some biscuits so I could sop them in butter and that ever-so-delicious Alaga Syrup we always had in the cabinet), and do my chores at my leisure.

It never worked, though. Guess whose idea trumped mine? Saturday chore times weren't up for discussion.

JEAN'S STEEP PRICE FOR DEFIANCE

When I last saw Jean that day, before what later became widely known as her "beak blunder," she was standing in our home's foyer, working mom's last nerve by playing with the umbrella. Mom demanded Jean take the umbrella outside because, according to her, it was bad luck to put it up inside the house.

Jean was still killing mom's juju when the unthinkable happened. Suddenly, the noises, made by the repeated open and close of the umbrella, stopped, but that's when the real sound effects exploded.

First it was just a whimper, a barely audible cry. But within seconds, Jean was screaming and hollering at the top of her lungs—and for good reason.

Blood was everywhere—and not just the thin liquid variety. I'm talking a gushing, flowing crimson river filled with thick clots of snot and human tissue. Down her shirt. Across the ceramic flooring. On the clear plastic of the umbrella. Everywhere.

Mom and Dad both rushed to Jean at once. Even I ran toward the pain-filled primal cries emanating from her lungs. And for a second, we all stood there in awe of the totally ridiculous sight before us.

Somehow, someway, that harebrained sister of mine had managed to get the metal pointy business end of that umbrella stuck three-inches deep into her right nostril. It was something only Jean could do.

Jean as a teenager, and without her fancy umbrella accessory.

After recovering from their initial shock, Mom and Dad immediately went into "let's get this umbrella out of this fool's nose" mode. All I was able to contribute was a wide-eyed, open-mouthed stare, a slow shake of the head, and a grin so wide my pearly whites could have lit up a small village. Dagnabbit! That was funny!

By this time, Jean was jumping up and down—completely panicked. To make matters worse, every time Mom and Dad tried to touch the umbrella, Jean yelled even louder, saying it hurt that much more.

All kinds of plans ensued: ease it out little-by-little, take her to the emergency room, or snatch it out quickly—Dad's method for removing all of our loose teeth.

The latter technique prevailed. Jean wouldn't stand still long enough for them to ease it out, and my parents just couldn't see themselves taking her all the way to the ER, enduring the incredulous stares of everyone there, and paying that huge hospital bill.

IF BRAINS WAS DYNAMITE, YOU COULDN'T BLOW YOUR NOSE

So, that's how it was done. Dad convinced Jean to close her eyes for just a moment and then gave that handle one big tug. Presto!

Thinking back, that fateful tug could have gone all sorts of wrong, but thank God it didn't.

Mom and Dad stopped the bleeding. Jean's nose was sore for a good little while, and it was a long time before she could even look in the direction of an umbrella without breaking into a cold sweat. Otherwise, she made a full recovery.

What she couldn't overcome, however, was the undeniable fact that she had achieved the goal she'd set before her. Her defiance had earned her the same accolades from Mom that, until then, had been solely reserved for me. Not long after everyone stopped shaking, Mom just had to say it. "Danggit, Jean, I told you to put that umbrella down. You have to be smarter than that. If brains was dynamite, you couldn't blow your nose!"

IF I TELL YOU A HEN DIPS SNUFF, YOU LOOK UNDER THE WING

Like many children, I was led by my own mind about nearly everything—my own opinions, my own ideas, my own thoughts. When people believed something different from what was rolling around in my head, from as far back as I can remember, I would challenge them to a hearty debate. If they were able to convince me their viewpoint made more sense than mine, I'd sometimes be open-minded enough to go with that. Sometimes.

If their logic fell short, well, that created a very serious quandary, which nearly always resulted in me claiming my original point superior to theirs and going about my business as usual. My mother called it "frustrating as hell," but I liked to think of it as simply being a confident, independent thinker. A leader, yes, and rarely a follower.

If Mom, like most moms, had her druthers, I would have taken her every word for the Gospel, abandon my own ideas, and assume hers were correct. But that was just not my way.

Often we'd go back and forth. Mom telling me her version. Me retorting. And then Mom finishing with these famous words: "Look Lita, why can't you just trust what I say? I don't care if something doesn't sound right to you. If I tell you a hen dips snuff, you look under the wing."

Most often, my propensity to lead produced decent results. Sometimes things went as planned; sometimes they didn't. But, rarely discouraged when things went awry, I'd just pick myself up, shake off the dust, and, like they say, try, try again....

On one occasion, however, trying again was simply out of the question. I had been beaten—badly—and the only thing left to do was surrender. Worse yet, I had to admit my mother's wisdom had been more prudent than mine. It truly was a day for the record books. Where were those Guinness folks when you needed them?

THOSE DARN SHOES

Quirky enough, it all started over a simple pair of shoes. I was a sixth-grader at Scott Elementary, a local public school that bordered our safe, tree-lined subdivision.

Because it was no more than a mile or so from our home, I, along with countless other friends, made that half-hour trek every Monday through Friday. I'd leave my home at about eight a.m. with just my younger sister, and (before long) our two-some would gradually grow to a ten-some as friends and classmates joined us along the way.

It was an easy walk. Evenly laid sidewalks led the entire way, watchful neighbors waved as we passed by, and dutiful crossing guards considered it an honor to ensure we navigated every intersection without incident.

When I first started that before-school routine, I was a gleeful kindergartner skipping and jabbering the entire way while clinging to my father's trusty hand. But as the years went by, and as I demonstrated more and more maturity, I graduated to the "big girl stroll" and was allowed to walk it alone. The independence was great, but it wasn't enough. I needed more affirmation that I had "arrived" as a soon-to-be middle schooler. I needed to schlepp around in big girl shoes.

As a scrawny little five-year-old with long but equally skinny feet, I was a Buster Brown and Stride Rite platinum status customer. They were the only brands with shoes that looked childlike, were extra narrow, and were long enough to ski on—all of which were requirements for my awkwardly growing feet.

Oh, and I needed shoes that didn't require a "real" heel in order to keep them on. The back of my lower leg, from my Achilles Heel to the soles of my feet, was one straight shot. No curves. No heel. Mom cursed this peculiar feature of my feet—the one she just knew was costing her extra money to fit.

Mom was a champion for well-made, good fitting shoes, so she took me where I needed to go and paid what needed to be paid. I believed it had something to do with her not having quality shoes when she was a kid, which resulted in her bad feet as an adult. I didn't really know for sure, and, as a kid, I can't say I even cared. All I was certain of was that while my sixth grade friends were strutting about in the latest styles and the flashiest kicks, I was stuck sloughing around in kiddy-looking orthopedic monstrosities. Needless to say, something had to change.

For some time, I had noticed the not-so-subtle differences between my shoes and those of my equally-cool friends. But, in my effort to pick my battles with my mom, I had mostly ignored the issue that I knew was sure to be a fight. Not that I was one for avoiding confrontation, but I had learned that I couldn't win them all. I had to let my mom win sometimes. It just kept the balance of real power secretly, and slightly, tilted in my favor—just the way I liked it.

The shoes were important, but there were bigger fish to fry. Things like frequently consuming candy and my expensive dental bills, carefully weaseling out of less-than-desirable chores, and quietly returning home just past the time our neighborhood streetlights illuminated. These were all must wins for me, so I let the shoes sit on the back burner for a while.

WEGGIE'S BIG PAY BACK

That all changed on a beautiful spring morning when I royally pissed off my younger sister, Weggie. The sun was out and our mid-Michigan weather was already about seventy-five degrees, so we were hanging around outside of our house waiting for 8:00 a.m. to roll around so we could begin our routine educational pilgrimage.

About five other friends were playing hopscotch with us on the sidewalk when Weggie got uncharacteristically snippy and accused me of cheating. Now that in itself should have told me this was unchartered territory, to be avoided at all costs, but back then I had never seen a fight I didn't like, especially if it came from the likes of my younger sister. I was eleven, she was nine, and I wasn't exactly a model big sister. Like most older and younger sibling relationships, she adored me. I was older. I was cooler. I mastered the lay of the land—especially around our mother. She worshiped me, but I barely tolerated her.

Now, truth be told, Weggie's foul mood didn't exactly begin when she accused me of cutting a few corners in that simple game of colored chalk, stones, and bunny hops. It actually began an hour earlier, before we had even breached the doors to the great outside.

Long ago, it had become a popular rule in our house that whoever turned on our family television first got to "own" it and watch what they wanted. Now this was important because we only had one television in our entire house—and Weggie and I had completely different tastes in programs.

She was a Rocky and Bullwinkle girl. She loved the cartoon's dim-witted moose and perky flying squirrel just as much as I hated them. Now, myself, I was a diehard Looney Toons fan. Foghorn Leghorn, Porky Pig, Daffy Duck, Bugs Bunny . . . now that was real comedy!

But most days it didn't matter. See, unlike me, Weggie was an early riser. Our mother would come into the room we shared every morning and gently shake each of us as we slept soundly in our twin beds decorated in every shade of pink, and with every bloom in the florist. It never failed that Weggie would jump up like a jack-in-the-box as soon as she heard Mom enter our room, while I would lay there like a drunken flounder, shamelessly begging for just ten more blissful minutes.

Lolita and Weggie cheesing for the camera during their elementary school years.

Shoot, before my feet ever hit the ground, Weggie would have already taken care of the bathroom necessities, gotten dressed, and been on her second helping of breakfast.

IF I TELL YOU A HEN DIPS SNUFF, YOU LOOK UNDER THE WING

Needless to say, she owned that doggone TV every single morning, which left me stuck watching Rocky and Bullwinkle try to outfox Boris and Natasha—and hating every second of it.

That particular morning, I'd had enough. So instead of sitting in the living room and seething like a storm cloud while watching that God-forsaken cartoon, I decided to do something about it.

Rules were rules, I knew that, but enough was also enough, and I just couldn't take it anymore. I couldn't watch another second of that ridiculous cartoon when I knew Daffy Duck was doing his best to outsmart Bugs Bunny. So, after breakfast, I slowly sashayed into the room with my hands stuck deep in my jeans pockets, walked over to the set while eyeballing my sister the entire way, and defiantly twisted the knob until I saw Bugs Bunny and Daffy Duck entangled in a heated argument about whether it was Rabbit season or Duck season. Classic!

Weggie was stunned.

My boldness had caught her off guard. She did all she could—called for Mom, tried to tell Dad—but in the end, they were both too busy to bother themselves with such trivial matters. That left me and Weggie—mano a mano—and, not surprisingly, I emerged the victor. But she wasn't happy.

After about a half hour, we went out to play. I was still reeling from the hilarious hijinks of Daffy and Bugs and had pretty much forgotten about our little spat, but it was still stuck in Weggie's craw. So, when she discovered my little cheating indiscretion, there was no way she was letting it go unnoticed.

She said I cheated at hopscotch. I claimed I didn't. And when it looked as if I was winning again, this time by persuading everyone else she was mistaken, she pulled out the big guns and said, "Well, that's why Mom makes you wear those ugly shoes!"

What followed was like a scene out of an old western. With those hateful words from Weggie, the world stopped. Nothing but loud gasps and then total silence followed.

Weggie's insult was a low blow, but well played. My shoes were indeed hideous, but they had absolutely nothing to do with hopscotch. Still, the damage had been done. Everyone had heard what she said, and I was utterly humiliated.

It was at that moment that I decided what had seemed insignificant before was no longer so. It was time to move the shoes all the way up on my priority list. It was time to have it out with Mom.

MAYBE I SHOULD HAVE LOOKED A GIFT HORSE IN THE MOUTH

Later that evening after dinner, I planned to tactfully broach the sensitive subject with Mom. I had it all carefully thought out in my head. This was a delicate matter, and I had only one shot. It had to be right. But somehow, once the conversation started, I cast subtlety to the wind, and it all just came tumbling out.

"I hate those shoes," I shouted. "Why can't I wear shoes like everyone else's? Everyone is making fun of me, even Weggie. Why can't I ever do what I want? You can't tell me what to do with my own money."

It was the last one that got to her. Mom was tired from teaching third graders all day, and she'd had her fill of me as well. I had come loaded for bear because this was something she felt strongly about, so imagine my surprise when after listening to my whining she simply said, "Okay."

But, as was her typical fashion, her concession was accompanied by her warning.

"Lita," she said, "be careful about what you buy. I know you have your eye on those shoes from Bakers Store, but you don't have Bakers feet. The wrong shoes are going to put a whupping on you. I can look at you and tell you're not listening, but you might want to pay attention this time. It's like I always say, if I tell you a hen dips snuff, you look under the wing."

And with that, she was done with it. She spun around and went about her business. And I went about mine—calling all of my girls and planning a shoe shopping trip for the weekend. I hadn't heard one single word my mom said, and she knew it. As she often put it, talking to me was like pouring water on a duck's back. It just wouldn't sink in.

I couldn't wait for the weekend. Mom had given me permission to buy my Bakers shoes, but she wouldn't go so far as to take me there to do it.

For that, I went to my other sister, Jean, who was four years my senior. The mall was actually closer to our home than my school, but getting to it required crossing a couple of busy streets without a crossing guard. We could go, Mom said, as long as Jean was with us.

Now Jean was about as accommodating to me as I was to Weggie. To her, I was the annoying little sister. But Jean was also quite enterprising. The path on her schedule was colored with green.

So after a bit of fierce negotiation, Jean agreed to take my crew and me to the mall—as long as we didn't take too long, as long as we listened and did exactly what she said, and as long as we didn't get on her nerves.

All I really heard was yada, yada, yada. But then she said yes, and promptly collected the five dollars we settled on.

THE BIG SHOPPING TRIP

I eagerly counted down the three days to Saturday by crossing each off with an X on my Pippi Longstocking wall calendar. When it finally arrived, I was up early, calling all of my girls to make sure they were still planning to meet at my house at 9:30 a.m. The mall didn't open until ten, but I wanted to be there when the employees unlocked and rolled up the steel gate guarding the entrance. Mine was a very detailed plan.

The fifteen-minute walk to the mall was full of chatter and excitement. Jean was bossy and impatient, but nothing she said or did could extinguish my exhilaration. I was about to cop my first pair of fashionable shoes. Everything was right with the world.

The walk seemed to take forever, so I was nearly beside myself when they finally opened the store. The bright lights looming overhead perfectly illuminated every single pair of shoes, amazing me with the beautiful sights.

I was aware of people nearby, but nothing really resonated. I was in a fairy tale, magically mesmerized while in that depository of flashy shoes like Hansel and Gretel were drawn into that home crafted from candy and gingerbread. But, little did I know that all was not well. Had I paid more attention to Mom, I would have known there was evil in that house of fashion. Podiatric evil.

After nearly an hour of methodically inspecting every single shoe on display, it was decision time. It's been forty years, but I can still see that shoe before me like it was yesterday.

I had admired all of my friends in platforms, so I decided early on that a wedge would serve as my main support. Eventually, I settled upon a real beaut. The shoe of my dreams started with a clunky tan cork wedge sole, which served as a steady foundation and boldly upheld a thick and slightly lighter-colored tan leather enclosure.

The top of the shoe had a rounded toe, coarse, dark brown stitching, and vertical gold grommets that housed woven mocha laces. It kind of resembled a brown leather platform tennis shoe, but better. Much, much better.

It was a shoe my mom never would have gone for, but this was not my mom's day. It was mine, and just the thought of me hoofing it around the playground in those babies made me as happy as a lark. I gladly handed the clerk twenty-five of my very own dollars and strutted right out that door. I wouldn't have been happier had someone just handed me the keys to my own candy store.

Don't let the million dollar smile fool you. When pushed too far, Weggie (here in elementary school) often had her way of leveling the playing field.

Most weeks I bemoaned the speed at which weekends flew by, but that Saturday and Sunday seemed to creep. I couldn't wait to show off my new kicks and planned my outfit down to the tiniest detail.

It all started with my favorite and most worn blue jeans and rounded out with my faded brown Scooby Doo t-shirt. Of course, it was all designed so the shirt and shoes would match. The only imperfection, which I convinced myself was ever so slight, was the back of the shoe. I just couldn't seem to keep it from slipping as I walked.

But, no matter. I had the perfect fix for that as well. To ensure a more snug fit, I put on my thickest pair of brown cotton socks and squeezed the rest of my foot in. I must admit it was a bit snug, but that was of no consequence. Nothing could stop my groove.

IF I TELL YOU A HEN DIPS SNUFF, YOU LOOK UNDER THE WING

TIME TO SHOW OFF MY NEW KICKS

That Monday morning was something special. Instead of waiting for mom to wake me up, I was roaming around the house, fully dressed, before she even came into our room. I was too excited to bother with breakfast, so I had gained full control of the TV before Weggie sprinted downstairs. There would be no Rocky and Bullwinkle that day, no sir. It was Daffy Duck all the way and, as usual, he was in rare form while trying to convince Porky Pig he "ought to be in pictures." Oh, no, Porky, I thought. It was me. I was the one worthy of Hollywood with my new kicks. Nothing could hold me back with those babies on.

After an hour or so yucking it up with Daffy and Porky, I headed outside to reveal "the shoes." When Weggie broke out the colored chalk in anticipation of hopscotch, I not-so-politely told her to think again.

Lolita and Weggie, 2015

The possibility of me scuffing up my new shoes was just too great. Instead, I chose to walk around, doing my absolute best to look cool, while everyone else stood around in awe. Or, at least, that's how I chose to think about it.

Most times, truth be told, you can see trouble coming a mile away. That was certainly true of my shoes, but, in my excitement, I chose to ignore the obvious signs.

The first one came almost immediately. I knew those shoes were too tight with my thick socks, but what else was I supposed to do? They just refused to stay up in the back, so I had to compensate for my non-heel. In any event, I was sure my leather upper would be broken in by the time I arrived at school, and then it would be a perfect fit.

IF I TELL YOU A HEN DIPS SNUFF, YOU LOOK UNDER THE WING

I couldn't have been more wrong. For the next eight hours, from 8:00 a.m. when I left home excited about my big debut, until 4:00 p.m. when I limped back totally defeated, those shoes whupped my butt.

There was no way I was ever going to admit it, but Mom had been right. For someone with feet like mine, there was a humongous difference between Stride Rite shoes and Bakers shoes.

Until that day, I had never imagined how much a shoe could hurt a foot—and how a pain that started in the feet could travel through the entire body. By the time I arrived back home, I was nearly crawling.

Running was out of the question, walking slowly only exacerbated the pain, even limping no longer worked. Dad had warned me about the dangers of walking outside barefoot, so that wasn't an option, either. That only brought visions of broken glass or rusty metals stuck deep under my tender skin, doctors with sharp instruments rooting it out, and long needles delivering tetanus shots.

By the time I arrived home, tears were streaming down my face. I don't think I could have taken one more step. Even my blisters had blisters. My feet felt like they had been stuck in a vise all day and were too sore to touch. Those little puppies were on fire.

When I was finally able to sit and peel back my thick socks, my poor feet revealed the trauma of a hardheaded little girl wearing ill-fitting shoes. There was nothing left to do but cry uncle and throw myself to the mercy of my younger sister.

God bless Weggie's soft heart. When she saw me sitting there in so much pain, she immediately went to the freezer and began rubbing ice on my swollen feet. I didn't have the words to express my gratitude, but I'm sure she felt it through the pained half-smile I was able to muster her way.

And, as luck would have it, guess who walked through the door shortly thereafter? Yep, it was Mom. When she first entered the living room with her purse still hung on her arm and a haggard look from a hard day's work, she didn't say a word. She just stood there and looked at Weggie sitting at my feet and the tears staining my face. It didn't take Sherlock, or Watson for that matter, to deduce what was going on.

I guess she figured I had already been punished enough, so she didn't say much. "So, you wore those shoes today, huh?"

With the most pitiful look I'm sure has ever graced my face, I nodded my head.

"Guess that didn't work out so well," she said as she walked away. And then I heard it. It wasn't loud, but it was definitely there. She couldn't resist. "If I tell you a hen dips snuff, you look under the wing."

= = = = = =
IT'S YOUR LITTLE RED WAGON—YOU CAN PUSH IT OR PULL IT

In our home, good grades were not a request; they were a requirement.

From as far back as I can remember, I was never asked if I would attend college. That was a given. My only choice was where. Mom and Dad made it abundantly clear that my two sisters and I could attend college anywhere we wanted, on their dime, but we had to go. And to get there, we were expected to earn excellent grades from elementary school all the way through the final day of high school.

Now for my two goody-two-shoes sisters, the grades weren't much of a problem. Although my eldest sister, Jean, was clearly the one who hated school most, there was one thing she despised even more: work. And Mom, of course, knew just what to do about that.

Whenever we had a day off from school, Mom took us with her so we could see what she did all day as a third grade teacher. To us, it looked like a walk in the park—Mom sitting behind a big metal desk while bossing little kids around. After a few hours, her students would leave the room for lunch and Mom would take us out for a bite to eat. Every now and then, they'd even come back from recess to watch a movie and eat snacks. Not bad.

That was Mom's job. Dad's was a bit different.

Dad, like so many others who worked in Michigan's automotive plants, had migrated from the south in the fifties to earn a comfortable living building Chryslers, Buicks, and Chevys. His work environment was as similar to Mom's as night and day, so we got to see them both.

The contrasts were striking. Mom sat behind a desk all day, while Dad stood on his feet. Mom worked six to seven-hour days, but Dad normally put in a minimum of eight. Mom worked Monday through Friday. With overtime, Dad often went in six or seven days a week. Mom was home for the entire summer and all holiday vacations, but Dad had to work.

All of that mattered, but, for Jean, the biggie was this: Mom's classroom was so orderly and quiet that she often joked you could "hear a rat piss on cotton." Dad's workplace at General Motors was just the opposite.

To discourage Jean from challenging the college edict, they told her it was either a post-high school education or a full-time job. And to make her decision easier, they made her accompany Dad to work on a couple of occasions.

Their tactic worked. Everything else set aside, Jean couldn't take the noise. The eight-hour, nonstop barrage of shrill metal grinding, high-pressure pumps, and industrial fans left her deafened and defeated. With or without earplugs, there would be no uprising. Jean gladly leaped onto the college bandwagon. For her, it was the lesser of two evils. She still hated school, but work had become completely out of the question.

Not surprisingly, after high school, Jean enrolled at Michigan State University and earned a couple of degrees in elementary education. Like Mom, she dedicated her life to teaching others.

Unlike Jean, I never questioned college, which is shocking, considering I challenged everything else. I drank every drop of that Kool-Aid. What I couldn't get down with was the "all A's, all the time" expectation. Now that was just too much.

So during the first marking period of seventh grade, my first year of junior high, I decided to dip my toe into the forbidden land of B's—just to see what would happen. Surprisingly enough, my defiance didn't rile Mom up as much as I feared. She just countered with her most serious, yet condescending, facial expression and cautioned me with her version of a subtle caveat.

"Okay, Lita," she said, "you know the rules. You're far too smart to bring penny ante grades into this house. But . . . it's your little red wagon. You can push it or pull it."

Then she took away a couple weeks of my television and outside play privileges.

No worries. I wasn't too torn up about that, mostly because I knew I was going to sneak them in anyway.

So, when I survived that mild scrimmage, I moseyed on into the sea of C's.

THE DREADED PARENT-TEACHER CONFERENCES

The day I received my first C was when I really discovered where Mom's line of tolerance ended. She hit the roof after attending second marking period parent-teacher conferences and seeing that C on my report card. Suffice to say, it was a full-blown conniption.

So, there I was, faced with the consequences of my own doing. I had gone too far, and Mom was beyond furious.

Math had never been my strongest subject, so it wasn't shocking that it was also not my favorite. It all started early in elementary school. I had a good time, but can't say I learned as much as I should have. Mom blamed most of it on

Mom, a former third grade teacher, in a school picture of her own.

the teachers' fondness of Quizmo. According to her, before junior high, the majority of my math instruction had come from the laminated cards stacked tightly inside the Quizmo game box. The rest of the problem, she insisted, could be attributed to my pure laziness.

Most of my friends didn't fully empathize with my unfair disadvantage when it came to educational matters. None of their parents were teachers, so their kitchen calendars didn't have every parent-teacher conference and every scheduled report card noted in thick red marker with bright yellow highlighted circles encasing them. Unfortunately for me, ours did.

Now, for my sisters, parental school visits didn't matter. They were pretty much going to walk the straight and narrow anyway. But, for me, that presented all sorts of difficulties.

IT'S YOUR LITTLE RED WAGON—YOU CAN PUSH IT OR PULL IT

First off, getting Mom to simply "forget" about a parent-teacher conference was out of the question. Only an act of God would have prevented her from attending every single one.

Secondly, she made it her business to be the first one there—fully armed with a list of questions prepared in advance, a fresh handout of warning signs designed to signal teachers I was about to "cut up" as she called it, and a contact sheet to arm teachers with every method known to God in which she could be reached. When it came to school matters, Mom left no stone unturned.

So, while my friends were busy distracting their moms and dads on parent-teacher conference days and manufacturing their own report cards, I was a sitting duck. As much as I hated it, those shenanigans were out of my reach. Mom would have smelled my "monkey mess," as she called it, a mile away.

LEST HISTORY REPEAT ITSELF

I knew I had messed up big time when mom saw my first C.

My first blunder was blowing off my teacher. He'd cautioned us that finding success in junior high school math would take more effort than we were expected to exert in elementary school—but who really listens to teachers? I just assumed it was something he was required to say, year after year, to all of the students. And since I was smarter than the average bear, his was a warning I need not adhere to.

My second faux pas was ignoring Mom's long-standing mandate that my sisters and I "beat bad news home."

Years ago, she had been mortified while attending a parent-teacher conference. Before leaving our house, she had asked me how I was doing in school, and if there was anything she needed to know before she got there. I gave her my standard answer of "everything's great," knowing full well that wasn't exactly the case.

Yes, my grades were fine, but I had gotten into a bit of trouble a few times leading up to the conference. Now normally, I was smart enough to be on my best behavior when I knew my mom would soon be visiting my teachers, but I had foolishly thrown all caution to the wind and continued to be the class chatterbox, even though my teacher had practically begged me to quiet down.

On one particular occasion, when my teacher was especially aggressive in her request, I slightly embarrassed her by snapping back that I was talking because I was bored—and if she were a better teacher, I would have been as quiet as a church mouse.

That's what brought me the real trouble. More than anything, I had challenged my teacher before her entire class, something my fellow students were quite delighted to see. Nevertheless, the teacher warned me that she would be talking to my mother about my fresh mouth. Now, in all fairness to me, I thought she meant she would be calling my mother that evening. And when the call never came, I assumed she had forgotten all about it and was willing to let bygones be bygones. Apparently not.

So, when my mother met with my teacher during conference time, she had no reason not to be in the best of moods. All the other teachers she visited that day had glowing reports about me, so she expected the accolades would continue. Only, they didn't, and Mom was livid.

That raw emotion stayed with her throughout the five-minute drive home, and there was hell for me to pay when she arrived. I knew as soon as she flung open the door that I had gone too far, but it was too late.

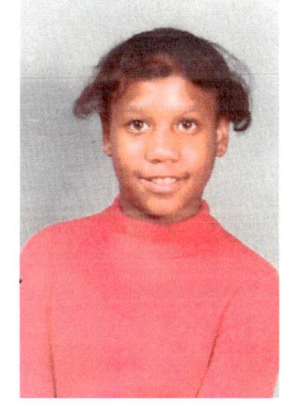

There was nothing for me to do but sit down, drop a few crocodile tears, and throw myself to the mercy of my mom. Problem was, I had gone to the goat house looking for wool (another one of her favorite sayings.) What I was seeking was simply not there. She was fresh out of mercy.

Not just leaning to the side, Lolita often ran outside of the house rules.

For my offenses, and her humiliation, I was sentenced to do everyone's household chores for a month, with no television, and no playing outside or having any friends over. Finally, she left me with strong advice.

"Next time," Mom said, "you'd better beat bad news home."

If there was troublesome news she should know, it had darn well come from me first.

IT'S YOUR LITTLE RED WAGON—YOU CAN PUSH IT OR PULL IT

THE AFTERMATH

So, when Mom returned home from my seventh grade parent-teacher conferences after learning I had earned a C in math, I didn't exactly have visions of lollipops and rainbows floating through my head. I knew she would be outraged. I had just underestimated to what extent.

With red eyes of rage and a voice filled with far more bass than usual, she ranted on and on.

"I told you a million times, Lita. It's your little red wagon. You can push it or pull it. Looks like you forgot how much harder it is to pull rather than push. So let me remind you. Remember when I said you could either think with your head or work with your back?

"Well, since you refuse to use your head, I'm going to help you strengthen your back," Mom continued. "From this day, until I tell you otherwise, every chore in this house belongs to you. And when you're done here, go next door and ask Mrs. Holland what you can do for her. And if you take even one thin dime from her for your work, you'll regret that for a good long time.

"You'll work from the time you finish your homework until the time you go to bed. On the weekends, it'll be from sun up until sun down. And since you want to play around in math class, I'm going to make sure you make up for it right here at home. Tomorrow I'm asking your teacher to give me every worksheet and every workbook he has. Trust me. When I'm done with you, math may not be your favorite subject, but you'll know it better than any other. You'll be doing those problems in your sleep. And if you even think about bringing another C into this house, I promise you, it'll be a day for your record books."

One thing I'll give to my mother, when she was pissed, she was a woman of her word.

Mom worked me like a Hebrew slave until the next report card came out—the entire three months. I cooked, I dusted, I scrubbed, I mopped, I vacuumed . . . I did it all. And if she ever felt badly for me, she never let it show. And, to really drive her point home, she'd occasionally walk by as the sweat was streaming into my eyes, just as it was putting me at risk of sudden blindness, mumbling, "Push it or pull it, push it or pull it." Did the woman know any mercy?

= = = = = =
LAZINESS WILL KILL YOU

It was a day that began like most others.

I was in middle school at the time, living in Michigan during one of the coldest and most miserable winters on record. The snow was raging out of the sky, accompanied by its equally malevolent chums—bitter temperatures and sneaky ice. Every time I ventured outside, I swore it would be my last until the first sign of spring.

What was I doing here? Even the birds had long abandoned this desolate place. Surely I was supposed to be smarter than them. But my dreams of leaving this God-forsaken land were short lived. Michigan was my home, and I was destined for an early death from freezing cold. Mother Nature was most certainly in a foul mood and determined to share her pain.

I was never a morning person, so I was still drowsy, half asleep, and feeling nasty as I prepared to leave for school at about 7:00 a.m. It was one of those days when Mom would say I had stickers in my pants.

As I slammed the front door to leave, I had five books in the fold of one arm because the black strap on my ratty ice-blue backpack had ripped from its base, and I had not yet mended it like my mother had asked me to do a couple of days prior.

When she told me to do it, I'm certain she knew, at the time, that her words were more of an exercise in futility than anything else. I nodded my head just enough to pacify her, but not enough to give her any level of confidence that I was actually going to move in the direction of the sewing kit.

We both knew what had not been said. I was definitely NOT going to repair that backpack anytime soon. And it was that silent acknowledgement that prompted her to look me in my light brown eyes and pronounce her familiar warning.

"Okay, Lita," Mom said. "Ignore me if you want, but one day, laziness will kill you."

That snow-covered school morning was also "band" day, so in addition to the burdensome pages of enlightenment bearing down on one arm, I was lugging and attempting to balance my long and bulky trombone in my other hand.

Yes, it was a bit much, but what's a girl to do? There were no other options. I HAD to carry my books that way because the backpack strap had snapped, and I HAD to carry that stupid trombone because I had begged my mother to buy it years earlier when I was in fifth grade.

See, my mother, knowing how fickle her daughter could be, wanted to rent the instrument, but that didn't sit well with me. I NEEDED to own my instrument, not blow into one that countless other cootie-carrying elementary school kids had deposited their hot breath into before.

So, we struck a compromise: she would purchase a brand spanking new trombone, and I would continue with band until high school. Thinking back, she really drove a hard bargain that day, and I was clearly slipping. She'd always wanted me to master an instrument, so she must have seen this as her golden opportunity.

I, on the other hand, was blinded by the shiny new brass instrument with all of its splendor, not realizing the lure of the brass would tarnish for me by the beginning of sixth grade. Yep, it was a sucker's deal solidified that day.

In any event, in our house, a deal was a deal, and I was a kid of my word. That meant I had to carry that huge monstrosity to school nearly every single day, even after I no longer had the slightest bit of interest in playing it.

Why wasn't I smarter in fifth grade? Why didn't I choose the flute with its petite little case—or better yet, why not percussion? All those guys ever had to carry was a couple of feather-light, easily concealed wooden sticks.

But oh, no, not me. I was one for doing it big. I just HAD to feel that cold slider between my fingers and pretend I was J.J. Johnson, one of the finest trombone players of all time. But, I digress . . . .

I was heading to the bus stop, wrapped up like a mummy in about five layers of clothing, loaded down with more than the law should have allowed. Dirty snow crunched under my feet with every step, and I continued to bemoan my heavy load just as much as the miserable cold.

Michigan Wonderland—that's what they had the nerve to call it. Michigan Wonderland, my foot. I had a few choice words for this place and with one look at my ice-covered nose hairs, runny nose, and red cheeks, no one needed "wonder" for long what they were.

The heavy trombone case was bad enough, but those darned books just refused to behave in my arm. Every time I took a step, one book would shift and jeopardize the whole load. It was like a house of cards just itching to collapse. I can't begin to express the relief I felt when I finally reached the bus stop without dropping a single hardback.

The bus ride to school was uneventful enough. It didn't take long before the bus sprang up to the front of the school, and I could see my perilous journey nearing its end. All I had to do was get inside to my locker, open the door slowly and carefully so all the crap I shoved in the day before didn't tumble out and crush me, hurl in four of the five books, and race to the band room to deposit my instrument.

Simple enough. Yes, both of my arms felt like noodles, but I was almost home free.

Shortly after the bus stopped, students jumped to their feet to exit at the front. I, on the other hand, knew the balancing act before me, so I decided to stay put until the aisle cleared.

That part worked well enough. But here's where I miscalculated: we were in the middle of a Michigan winter, Wonderland no less, and Mom had already given me fair warning—laziness would kill me.

Sure enough, as soon as I passed by the bus driver and maneuvered down the three steps, my right foot landed directly onto a patch of translucent, slick, sneaky-as-all-get-out ice.

It was one of those horrible moments when all of your thoughts come to you at once and you just know that nothing good can come from it.

See, as I wrestled to balance that couldn't-be-more-unbalanced trombone and

LAZINESS WILL KILL YOU

those five books, I skated around that ice looking like a cross between James Brown and Michael Jackson—with, mind you, about 200 middle school students mesmerized by my saucer-sized eyes, horrified expressions, and wild gyrations.

And during all of that time, the most prevalent thought in my head was that of my mom telling me days before to mend my backpack. With every slide this way, and attempt to regain my balance that way, I could still hear her words reverberate in my mind, "Okay, Lita, but one day laziness will kill you."

How could she have possibly known that my failure to do what she asked would make me the laughing stock of Whittier Junior High for days to come? How could she have known that I'd be continuously taunted with imitations of my dance on the ice that were so funny even I finally had to laugh?

I wasn't nearly ready to subscribe to the old "mama knows best" school of thought, but for one millisecond I actually considered the possibility. It would be years before I fully grasped the enormity of a mother's intuition and wisdom. But before that happened, I must admit that every time I felt the temptation to overload myself for the sake of "saving a trip," I remembered Mom's warnings. It scared the bejeebers out of me. And even though I wasn't always dissuaded, I did proceed with caution. I wonder . . . was she expecting any more than that?"

= = = = = =
I'VE ALREADY FALLEN OUT OF THAT TREE YOU'RE TRYING TO CLIMB

By now, it's been firmly established that, as a kid, I was no stranger to trouble. I got into it coming and going. But there was also an abundance of occasions when I was busy planning my next caper, wheeling and dealing, shucking and jiving—and, just when I was about to pull the trigger, my mom would let me know the jig was up.

It was then that Mom would say, "Come on, Lita, I already know what you're up to. Watch yourself, now. I know you don't believe fat meat is greasy, but I've already fallen out of that tree you're trying to climb."

And then I'd know for sure. I was busted. So there would be only one move left to make: covertly call my partners in crime and whisper, "Abort. Abort. Plan A's a bust . . . so it's time to move on to B."

Giving up was NEVER an option.

Unfortunately for me, there was one occasion (actually numerous ones) when I should have tucked my little tail between my little legs and gone for the early surrender. Doing so would have preserved my freedom and left my summer vacation intact. But that would have been the easy route. That would have been booorrrring. Instead, I chose the full-steam-ahead route.

Late May/early June marked the near-end of our school year—and that's when the natives began to get restless.

Valencia Sanders, my best friend from first grade, was my ace. She was a year older and a grade higher than I, but neither of those facts mattered. We were alike in every way and shared a relationship closer than most sisters.

Val and I both grew up on the same street and were inseparable. We walked to school together, went to dances together, had sleepovers together, and, yes, often schemed together. Mom called us Mutt and Jeff. Until recently when I researched the reference, I never even knew what that meant. But, because Mom said it when Val and I looked suspicious for one reason or another, I pretty much knew it referred to the pejorative.

Don't get me wrong. Mom loved Val as much as she loved Jean, Weggie, and me. Similarly, I was always welcome at Val's house. But our parents had been kids at one time themselves, so they always saw trouble coming, and Val and I often looked, as Mom put it, "like the back end of bad luck." You know what they say, "Game recognizes game."

It was early June 1980, my first year in the big leagues at Central High School and Val's second. She had already uncovered and conquered the lay of the land by the time I arrived, which made for an unusually smooth transition for me.

We'd spent most of the school year being good girls—getting the grades required by our parents, running on the varsity track team, and staying out of trouble—so that left plenty of room to have some real fun.

The school year was scheduled to wind down in a week or so, and most of the teachers and students were already in summer vacation mode (in their minds, anyway). There wasn't a whole lot left to do before the official last day of school arrived, so Val and I were bored.

I'd heard Mom quote the old English proverb time and time again that an idle mind is the devil's playground, and boy she wasn't joking.

One day after school, Val and I discussed our "situation:" how there was so little left to do in school, and, if there was something remaining, we weren't all that interested in it anyway.

That agreement led to a bigger question: what should we do? Our search for that answer took a variety of twists and turns that day, but we ultimately settled on a caper that excited us both: skipping school and spending the day at

Flint Northwestern High. After all, that was an excursion that had it all—disobedience, adventure, and, most of all, excitement.

See, Central and Northwestern were on the opposite ends of town, and Val and I had both been specifically ordered by our parents to stay on our side of town. The mere fact that we were thinking about disobeying our parents only added to the allure, which made Northwestern the perfect destination.

After a short bit of logistical planning, it was all set. Instead of attending our classes at Central the following day, Val and I would bless the poor schmucks trapped within the cement block walls at Northwestern with our glorious presence. Oh, this was going to be good. It was an ingenious plan, not because we'd simply be skipping school, which for most others would be bold enough, but our plan was far more complicated and held far more intrigue.

Neither Val nor I had a car yet, so transportation was definitely an issue. But, Val, being the worldlier of our little duo, worked us through that minor snafu. We'd get on just the right city bus, at just the right bus stop, at just the right time, and bingo! We'd be at Northwestern in no time.

All the while she yammered on about that, I just listened because it was waaaaay out of my wheelhouse. City buses had been off limits to me my entire life, so I knew absolutely nothing about them. Mom and Dad had forbidden me from riding on one, warning that I might get lost, but that only made me want to check them out even more. I was fifteen years old and had never ridden a city bus in my entire life. Of course, the thought of doing so added an extra glimmer in my eye.

Valencia Sanders, Lolita's partner in crime. Her ace!

Neither of us had any idea what we'd do when we arrived, but Val did have a few friends at Northwestern, so we silently assumed we'd look them up.

I'VE ALREADY FALLEN OUT OF THAT TREE YOU'RE TRYING TO CLIMB

Haphazardly, we gave no attention to the fact that we didn't know what classes they'd be in when we arrived. That was a minor detail, one that would not be allowed to curtail our plans.

For me, none of it mattered. Val had me at the mere mention of "city bus." And the reality that I was going on this adventure with her, and not my parents, was icing on the cake.

That next morning, as I pretended to prepare for a ho-hum day at Central, but secretly got ready for my big adventure at Northwestern, Mom seemed uncharacteristically quiet.

Normally, she was a chatterbox. I always believed my mom would talk to a dead tree if she suspected it would respond, but not that morning. She was still pleasant, but more reserved—definitely unlike her usual self. But, not normally one to focus on the superfluous, I paid little attention.

More often than not, Mom drove me to school, and in the car that day, I could hardly contain my excitement. I laughed loudly at every joke told on the radio, fidgeted with my clothes incessantly, and chewed my gum especially hard and fast. It was the beginning of a banner day. I could just feel it.

When we entered the parking lot, and I opened the door to pop out of the vehicle, Mom quickly grabbed my left arm and said the words I least wanted—and expected—to hear.

"Watch yourself today, Lita," she said. "You know what I always tell you. I've already fallen out of that tree you're trying to climb."

Really? Really? Was she kidding me? How could she have possibly known? And then it came to me.

Val and I had mapped out our entire plan while hanging out on my deck the day before, which, by the way, was located underneath the kitchen window where my mother was preparing dinner. Why it didn't occur to either Val or me that my mother might be doing a bit of ear hustling, I do not know.

We were smart girls, but, more importantly, we were cautious girls, especially when it came to keeping our nosy parents out of our business. Maybe it was the heat that day. After all, it was June in Michigan, a state prone to the most extreme weather conditions imaginable. Cold as a well digger's tail in the winter and hot as Hades in the summer. Crap! Once again, Mom had gotten the drop on me.

I'VE ALREADY FALLEN OUT OF THAT TREE YOU'RE TRYING TO CLIMB

But it didn't matter. Not this time. That train was already barreling down the tracks, and I wasn't about to lift a finger to stop it.

So what did I do next? The only logical thing: I played dumb and insisted I didn't have the slightest idea what my mother was talking about. She didn't buy it, though. She never did. Instead, she gave me a dry "um-hum," released my arm, and slowly drove away while staring back in her rearview mirror.

A couple of minutes later, Val and I met up outside the school and headed for the nearest bus stop. We were both on cloud nine. We chatted the entire half-mile or so.

First thing she asked was if I remembered my coins for the bus fare.

"Yep," I said, "took 'em out of my piggy bank last night."

From there, we talked about what we were going to do at Northwestern, who we might see, who might see us, and what we'd eat later in the day.

I must say the whole city bus thing was kind of a letdown. Completely uneventful. People got on. People got off. It just made me wonder why I was so determined to ride on it. The only noteworthy part was the smooth ride. Whereby school buses seemed to get lost in potholes and grind their way out, city buses just glided right over those bad boys and added a bounce to boot. Those babies knew how to float.

When we arrived at Northwestern, classes were in session, so no one was outside.

Right away, I noticed the difference in architecture. Central, built in the early 1920s, was the Flint Schools' first building, and it appeared so. The three-story red brick monstrosity looked, and felt, old. Northwestern, by contrast, wasn't exactly shiny, but it was definitely newer. Built in 1964, Northwestern was a one-story sprawling building that boasted its air-conditioning, pool, and the best track in the county.

Val and I had not traveled across the city to study exterior designs, so we quickly walked inside. And this is when things really got interesting.

Immediately upon entering, we walked down a hallway or two, peeking into classroom windows as we went along. Val noticed a few familiar faces, so she waved quietly, trying not to make too much noise. She motioned to a couple friends that we would be in the hallways when class let out, so we could get together then.

We were probably in the building for about five minutes when the bell rang, indicating it was time to change classes. At the first hint of that familiar sound, everyone came rushing out into the hallways.

For the next four minutes, Val and I had a grand old time. She saw people she knew. I saw a few I knew, and everyone was glad we were there. That whole skipping school thing made us look cool, and we reveled in every second of it.

But good things never last for long. Someone who identified himself as the principal soon spoke over the loud speaker, announcing the beginning of a hall sweep and that everyone had two minutes to get into his or her next class. What? Hall sweep? What the heck was that?

Unfortunately, Val and I learned quickly that what they didn't do at Central they did quite regularly at Northwestern. Unannounced hall sweeps were their attempt to keep uninvited visitors out of the school.

It was almost like a game of student musical chairs. After that two-minute warning, administrators combed the building, and every Northwestern student found roaming the hallways, instead of inside a locked classroom, was taken to the principal's office.

Lolita, Val's partner in crime!

Even worse for us, every non-Northwestern student found roaming the hallways, instead of inside a locked classroom, was taken to the truancy officer's office where unspeakable consequences awaited. Val and I found all of that out in short order as our friends rushed to get to their next classes. We could tell this was serious business when we realized their need to get to class was

I'VE ALREADY FALLEN OUT OF THAT TREE YOU'RE TRYING TO CLIMB

far more urgent than their need to spend time with friends who had just traveled across the city to visit them.

Crap! What were we supposed to do?

We didn't have a "next class" to get into. All the exterior doors to the school had been locked. And sneaking into a classroom was out of the question, as every teacher stood outside his or her classroom admitting only the proper students and locking the door at the appointed time. How were we going to get out of this one?

Thank God Val possessed both beauty and brains. I stood there frozen, just imagining how much trouble awaited me when the truancy officer called my mother (a long-time educator in the Flint School district) and explained that not only was I skipping school, but I also had taken the city bus for miles, and been careless enough to get caught up in a hall sweep. It was all too much. Shock had set in. I was a goner.

When my mind returned to my body, I realized Val was practically dragging me down the hallway while peeking into every classroom until she found just the right one.

She never flaunted it, but Val knew she was a looker, and that her beauty was the best weapon she could count on to get us out of our mess. Val was about five feet and ten inches tall, 125 pounds, with long flowing hair, glowing brown skin, and a smile that would melt an ice castle in seconds. Drop dead gorgeous, that girl.

Mom, not believing a word of the story

Finally, Val spotted her mark—a male teacher who looked friendly enough to be mesmerized by her exquisiteness and softhearted enough to show us some much needed mercy and compassion. Within seconds, he was charmed and we were safe.

That ride back home was a whole lot different from the ride there. Our faces were long, and neither of us spoke barely a word. Except for the way we were dressed, anyone observing us would have guessed we'd just left a funeral. And that's pretty much how I felt.

I had been so afraid during that hall sweep that I think a bit—just a smidgen—of my adventurous spirit floated away that day. I realized Val was just as traumatized when she didn't even suggest we stop for lunch on the way back. Normally, Val and food were synonymous, but that day, even vittles didn't matter.

Val and I doubled back to Central in plenty of time to catch a couple of our own classes and return home to pretend we'd had another ordinary, humdrum day.

The entire time, all I could think about was the ominous warning Mom had given me earlier that day. I even imagined how much trouble I would have been in if she had any idea what I'd done—and then I thanked God for the teacher who let us into his classroom and the fact that Mom didn't have a clue.

When Mom came home that afternoon, I was sitting in my room, still reeling from the scariest day I'd ever had. I'd gone awry often enough, but being nearly detained by a truancy officer was the closest I'd come to any involvement with the law—and the thought of that rattled me to my core.

So, when Mom waltzed into my room, I was nicer than usual about her uninvited presence in my personal space—mostly because of the safety and security she represented.

For a couple of minutes she talked about everything and nothing, and then she asked about my day.

I hesitated for a moment, not to consider actually telling the truth, but just long enough to wonder how much she already knew.

After quickly convincing myself I was being both paranoid and silly, I gave her my standard, "It was okay," response. She didn't normally get anything more than that, so I didn't think that day should be any different.

"Hmmm," Mom said. "That's strange, because my community school director friend at Northwestern said he could pretty much swear he saw you and Val over there today. But, I guess that wasn't you. Huh?"

My life flashed before my eyes—or at least the two days prior. My mind was racing. How much had she heard from the window? Did her friend really see us, or was she bluffing? She'd done that before, and she was pretty good at it. Was she doing it again? Had she called Central and learned we weren't there most of the day? What did she actually know?!

I hesitated before responding because Mom was really good at these little skirmishes, mostly because she could be so patient.

I rarely told the truth during these times, and she suspected me, but it could be tough to tell. I always went for the reasonable doubt. My overriding thought was to pick a cunning lie, stick with it, and then shut up.

On the rare occasions Weggie and Jean actually did anything wrong, they'd trap themselves up by telling five different stories for one series of events. Mom would ask them a few more questions, and they'd get nervous and change their stories. Then they'd add details. Then they'd talk some more. Before they knew it, they often talked themselves straight into a punishment that could have been avoided with one quick story followed by silence.

My technique called for giving as few details as possible, sticking to the original story, and then clamming up. Worked like a charm.

But that day was different. Too much trauma. I was off my usual game. That day I actually wanted to tell the truth, but, in the end, it just wasn't in me.

So, when Mom said her friend saw me at Northwestern that day, I countered with a fresh-mouthed, "Well, he must need glasses."

But as soon as it came out of my mouth, I knew she had the whole story. I could see it in her face. A mix of anger, disappointment, and excitement for finally "hemming me up," as she called it.

The next thing she did was pretty much lay out every step Val and I took as soon as we walked through the front doors of Northwestern High.

As it turned out, she had heard every detail of the plan Val and I discussed on the deck and alerted her friend, who worked in the building, to be on the lookout for us the following day.

Shoot, from all he reported to her, he had to have been waiting for our arrival all morning. One would think he would have had better things to do. Unfortunately, for me, he didn't.

The rest was pretty standard: a long lecture about my refusal to follow the rules and her fear for my personal safety, yada, yada, yada, no going anywhere for a month, blah, blah, blah, no friends over for a month (including—and especially—Val), yada blah yada blah, hard labor with doing everyone's chores for a month, yada blah yada blah.

I will say, however, that the entire experience made me see Mom a little differently that day. It wasn't quite enough to put me on the straight and narrow, but even I had to admit—if only to myself—that Mom's actions had touched my heart.

Before, I saw her interference into my affairs as nothing more than the nosiness of an overzealous old woman who was looking for any and every opportunity to bring upon me the wrath of God. This time, however, recent events enlightened me. I couldn't ignore all of the trouble she had gone through to ensure I would be safe when I stepped into that school. I even found out later that the "random" hall sweep that day wasn't just a stroke of bad luck, after all. Mom's friend had lost track of Val and me, so he orchestrated the entire thing to bring us back to safety.

For all I know, Mom even had someone disguised as an anonymous rider on the bus looking out for our wellbeing. I wouldn't have put it past her.

The bottom line was that I was finally coming to the realization that my mom loved me deeply and, as desperately as I sometimes wanted to believe otherwise, her actions reflected that.

Now, don't get me wrong. I only had a slight change of heart—not a complete case of the body snatchers. Like I said before, giving up was NEVER an option.

But, I took great pleasure in the fact that Mom decided against telling Val's mom what we'd been up to that day. She never said why, and Val and I dared not ask. We'd learned long ago that it just wasn't smart to look a gift horse in the mouth, but we used that little opening for our benefit as well.

Throughout my thirty-day sentence on "the rock," Val utilized her freedom to sneak me bits of information so I'd know what was going on in the neighborhood. She even brought me penny candy and helped with my chores when Mom and Dad were away. A true friend Val was—and still is to this day.

\======

CHECK THE OIL, NOT THE GAS, 'CAUSE SOME THINGS WILL TAKE CARE OF THEMSELVES

Mom's words of wisdom eventually had just the effect I'm sure she was seeking all along.

After years of listening to, mocking, and then learning from her quirky sayings, they eventually became a part of my sisters and me. And as we grew, somehow the dictums we hated so much became undeniably interwoven into our DNA. So much so, in fact, that we'd catch her eccentric caveats emanating from our own mouths as warnings to our own children when they misbehaved.

At first, we were chagrined to think we had become our mother. But after a while, we stopped fighting the "I am not my mother" feminine crusade and accepted it all as pure fate. After all, her words and predictions had proven true time and time again—until we had become the kind, responsible, decent human beings she had envisioned for us all along.

Jean, the eldest, was the first of us to give Mom and Dad a grandchild.

Johnathan was born in June of 1983 and came into this world full of ideas that were all his own—and strong-willed enough to see them through. At the ripe age of nine months, it was quite apparent that his personal motto was "consequences be damned." Regardless of the redirection, praise, or discipline administered, Johnathan was going to do whatever Johnathan decided to do—and that was simply that.

Jean often said there must have been some sort of mix up. With his personality—a combination of stubbornness, tenaciousness, persistence, and pure imagination—Jonathan was most certainly supposed to be my child, not hers.

My firstborn came in 1988, after my then-husband, Jerry, and I had been married five years.

Briana quickly became the joy of our lives—and her temperament the spitting image of mine. Jerry, whose personality was pleasantly mild-mannered and conciliatory, often said he was being punished for my previous sins.

From the moment Briana's disposition began to emerge, it was evident that she was determined to test all limits.

She was bossy, outspoken, and opinionated. Yep, she was mine all right—a chip off the old block. It did Mom's heart good to see Briana challenge my authority. She said it was my penance—I was "paying for my raising."

Jerry, who had grown up a near-perfect child, didn't quite know what to do with her. But I did. I remembered exactly what worked best with me—lots of love, discipline, and constant correction—but, every now and then, an aloof eye. During those times, I remembered what Mom would occasionally remind herself out of exasperation, "Check the oil, not the gas, 'cause some things will take care of themselves."

That particular phrase really came in handy for me during the summer of 1999.

Johnathan turned sixteen that year and was giving Jean and her husband, John, the business like never before. He didn't do anything criminal. It was all just petty offenses like correcting his report cards when his teachers "carelessly" recorded grades lower than what he knew his parents would find acceptable, or sneaking out of the house at night to party with friends, but misjudging how far down it was when he climbed out of his bedroom window, slipping on the roof and landing on the pavement two stories below. For that bit of tomfoolery, he was rewarded with a torn meniscus that he still suffers from today.

CHECK THE OIL, NOT THE GAS, 'CAUSE SOME THINGS WILL TAKE CARE OF THEMSELVES

But the straw that broke the camel's back was his incessant request to shave his head. I still do not know to this day why that nut got it into his mind that shaving his head at sixteen would make him look cooler. But, of that, he was sure, and no one could convince him otherwise. For Johnathan, there were no alternatives. It had to be done.

In any event, the tension in their home was clearly at its breaking point, so Johnathan asked if he could live with me for the remainder of the summer. After all, I lived just across town, a mere ten minutes away.

It took only a few hours for me to consider the request and conclude a little distance might do them all some good. I later spoke to Jean and John, and we all agreed it wasn't a bad idea. That same day, Johnathan excitedly packed his bags and eagerly moved in with us.

BE CAREFUL WHAT YOU ASK FOR

When Johnathan arrived, I sat him down and laid out all of the rules. No missing curfew, no cursing, no drinking, no drugs, no sloughing around, and the like. He convinced me that none of those would be a problem, which wasn't a hard sell because Johnathan really was a good kid. But, true to form, he didn't make it to the end of day one before asking if he could shave his head.

Oh, crap, I thought. Here we go. Jean's battle is now my war. What was I thinking when I said I'd help raise a rebellious teenager for an entire summer?

I had known all along that Johnathan's personality was equally yoked with mine. I was now old enough to realize what that meant and the magnitude to which I had driven my own mother absolutely nuts while I was growing up. Charity was one thing, but this was just downright foolish. Why had I done such a thing?

And then I remembered Mom's approach when all else had failed—and when the worst possible consequence was not a life or death issue. I closed my eyes and visualized her walking through the house muttering, "Check the oil, not the gas, 'cause some things will take care of themselves." And, for the first time ever, I could see the sly smile on her face every time she said it., the slightly turned up lips on the left side of her face. How could I have missed that before? Had she seen the outcome every time she retreated into that last resort? Had my outcome been that obvious? Oh, Lord, I sure do hope not.

CHECK THE OIL, NOT THE GAS, 'CAUSE SOME THINGS WILL TAKE CARE OF THEMSELVES

"Hey, Aunt Leet," Johnathan called out to me shortly after unpacking. ("Leet" was a nickname everyone in the family had grown fond of. I never knew where it came from, and surprisingly enough, I don't remember ever asking. All I know is if someone said, "Leet," I answered. It was a rare form of indifferent obedience for me.)

"Yeah, honey, what is it?" I asked, but, truth be told, I knew full well what that boy wanted before he had gotten my name out.

"Can I shave my head?"

"Why . . . why do you want to shave your head, Johnathan?"

"I don't know. I just want to. Can I do it?"

"Didn't your mama tell you no?"

"Mama ain't here. You said I have to follow your rules while living under your roof. So, can I shave my head?"

"I don't know, Johnathan. I don't know if that's a good idea."

"Why, Aunt Leet? Why isn't it a good idea? Mama always said no, but when I asked 'why,' she just said, 'because I said so.' But that's not a reason, so why can't I shave my head?"

"Well, Johnathan, I just have two questions."

Briana and Johnathan looking good, but always up to something.

"What are they, Aunt Leet?"

"Did your mama ever tell you about her labor with you?"

"What do you mean?"

"Did your mama ever tell you she was in hard labor with you for nearly twenty-four hours and that your stubborn little tail didn't want to come out?"

"Maybe. I don't know. But what does that have to do with me shaving my head?"

CHECK THE OIL, NOT THE GAS, 'CAUSE SOME THINGS WILL TAKE CARE OF THEMSELVES

"It has EVERYTHING to do with your head, Johnathan. Think about it, son. Your mother pushed for hours to get you to come out, which means you were in the birth canal for a long, long time."

Johnathan looked at me like I had hopped down some rabbit trail that was as far off the topic of our conversation as I could possibly go. And then he said, "Look, Aunt Leet, I don't know what you're talking about. Now can I go shave my head?"

"Johnathan, come on now. Use your brain, son. You were stuck in the birth canal for hours, and that's a tight spot. It's really narrow in there, very narrow."

"Soooo…?"

"Soooo, when you finally came out of there, it looked like your head had been squeezed between two vices. You ever wonder why I sometimes call you 'long head'?"

"Ha. Ha. Funny. Funny, Aunt Leet. Now you're just trying to make fun of me."

"I'm telling you, Johnathan, you have hair on your head now, but the last time I saw it bald, it wasn't a good look. Are you sure you want to sport your dome without any covering?"

"Okay, Aunt Leet, okay. So now you got jokes, huh? You already know my head looks good. It's a part of the rest of me, ain't it?"

"Yeah, yeah, whatever," I countered in my most mocking tone. "But I do have just one more question, Johnathan. How are you going to shave it? I'm not paying for a barber to do it, and I know for sure your parents aren't, either."

Now that question caught Johnathan totally off guard. He'd never gotten that far with his mom before, so he hadn't worked out the particulars.

But, that's when his ever-so-eager cousin, Briana, jumped to his rescue. She had been avidly watching our entire exchange, head moving back and forth as if she was seated in the front row of the championship game at Wimbledon.

She and Johnathan were kindred spirits, and she wanted to learn from a true master. Johnathan was five years older than Briana, and she knew he was far more advanced in the manipulation of parents, so she considered this an

CHECK THE OIL, NOT THE GAS, 'CAUSE SOME THINGS WILL TAKE CARE OF THEMSELVES

impromptu advanced crash course. She'd been sitting there quietly the entire time taking copious notes.

"I'll do it for him," Briana said quickly and excitedly. "I'll shave Johnathan's head."

"Yeah, Aunt Leet," Johnathan seconded right away, catching up to Briana's "hair-brained" scheme. "Briana's gonna do it, so I don't need a barber."

"Hmmmm . . . so you don't need a barber, huh? Well, this ought to be interesting," I said with that same sly smile I had seen on my mom's face over the years. "Go ahead then, you two. Just be careful. Those razors can be really sharp."

Soon after they had disappeared into the bathroom, I called Jean to update her on the events of the day.

"You did what?" she asked in a shrill voice brimming with annoyance and anger. "I've been telling that boy for more than a year he couldn't shave his head, and, on day one, you just go ahead and let him do it? I know he's living with you for a while, but why Leet? Why would you do such a thing?"

"Now wait, Jean," I implored. "Just hear me out. Johnathan's been begging you for a whole year to shave his head, and all you've done is say no. But where has that gotten you?"

"Yeah, so what gives you the right to backdoor me and let him do it?"

"Nothing, but think about this. Remember when we used to bug Mom until she got so tired she'd just say, 'go ahead, 'cause some things will take care of themselves'?"

"Ooooohhhh," Jean said, slowly coming around to see my point.

"And listen to this, 'cause it gets better. Your genius son said he doesn't need a barber. Briana's gonna do it for him."

There was silence for a moment—and then the laughter came. And it came. And it came. Jean cackled for nearly two minutes straight. She said she had tears streaming down her face and cramps in her sides. Finally, she composed herself long enough to laugh aloud, "Just call me when they're done. I can't wait to see it!"

CHECK THE OIL, NOT THE GAS, 'CAUSE SOME THINGS WILL TAKE CARE OF THEMSELVES

It didn't take long. I guess Johnathan had Briana start right away before I had a chance to change my mind. Little did he know that all the gold in Fort Knox couldn't have persuaded me to tell him no. This was going to be a great lesson for both of my little hellions, and a perfect way to start our little summer camp.

LESSON LEARNED

Let's just say the entire ordeal was "bumpy" from start to finish—the beginning was figurative and the ending literal.

Johnathan, years later in high school, after vowing to never shave his head again.

Neither Briana nor Johnathan knew the best shaving tool, so they settled upon the disposable Gillette razor I used to shave my armpits.

Then, once Briana started to shave without any lubricant or cream—and Johnathan started to moan from the discomfort—they switched to Irish Spring soap, thinking that would make an ideal substance. Despite its "fresh and clean" scent, they discovered later that it wasn't so ideal after all.

As one might imagine, their euphoric moment of victory didn't last long. When they came back into the room, Johnathan was a bloody mess. And, again, that's literal.

Briana, the eleven-year-old non-expert head shaver that she was, had nicked and gashed that boy's head from front-to-back and side-to-side. There was no place on his head without the tell-tale signs of her exuberance and inexperience—except where there were untouched patches of hair remaining. Apparently once a spot became too tender, Johnathan begged her to simply move on to another area of his head.

CHECK THE OIL, NOT THE GAS, 'CAUSE SOME THINGS WILL TAKE CARE OF THEMSELVES

When it was all done, he looked like he had been attacked by the most severe case of scalp ringworm on record, and then sat in the chair of a barber who was drunk, high, and secretly pissed off.

When they came back into the room, there was not even one hint of the boldness and defiance from before.

Johnathan was certainly the more injured of the two, but they were both a pitiful looking mess. Briana was tearful and apologetic for the horrible job she did with her cousin's hair, and Johnathan was just in straight-up pain.

While his mother was across town unable to maintain her composure after hearing about his half-baked plan, he was standing before me begging for pain cream and someone to "fix" his hair.

I wanted to laugh (I really did), but I just didn't have the heart. His lesson had been learned, so it was time to show them both who was really in charge by taking control and fixing the "hairy" mess they had made.

I started by spreading Neosporin ointment on his head full of cuts and using scissors to remove as much of his remaining hair as possible. I dared not further the damage by shaving even more hair – plus I wanted some of the hair to be an embarrassing reminder of why he should have listened to his parents in the first place.

And then I dropped the real bomb: the worst was yet to come.

See, neither Briana nor Johnathan knew about the African American man's struggle with razor bumps. They didn't know that most black men don't use razors on their faces or heads because of their tendency to create ingrown hairs and scars.

Unfortunately for Johnathan, he was about to find out. Just a few days later, Johnathan's plight went from "I can't stand this" to "somebody please just chop off my head." His entire scalp was covered in nasty, pus-filled razor bumps and ingrown hairs. It even got so bad that I had to take him to the emergency room one night for the pain and infection.

So, between the "I told you so's" from his parents, ridicule from his friends, and pain from the scars, I never, ever had to worry about Johnathan begging to shave his head again. He and Briana had learned their lesson.

CHECK THE OIL, NOT THE GAS, 'CAUSE SOME THINGS WILL TAKE CARE OF THEMSELVES

As a matter of fact, the entire ordeal made them both a little nervous anytime I relented too quickly on any of their requests.

They'd ask, "What? What? Is this small stuff? Is this something that's gonna take care of itself?" And every time, instead of answering, I'd just walk away, whispering to myself, "Thank you, Mom."

CHECK THE OIL, NOT THE GAS, 'CAUSE SOME THINGS WILL TAKE CARE OF THEMSELVES

= = = = = =

IT'S GONNA BE TEDDY AND THE BEAR—AND THE OLD BEAR'S GONNA BE ON TOP

Jean's second child, Jared, came along four years after her first, and was cut from the exact same cloth she'd been patterned from nearly thirty years earlier.

Born in 1987, he arrived docile and mild-mannered, just as Jean has been the majority of her life. There was not a sweeter kid in all the land.

Still today, I vividly remember his four-year-old response when anyone asked what he wanted to be when he grew up. Most children quickly rattled off all kinds of grown up professions like doctors, lawyers, and teachers, but not Jared. For about two years, until he was shamed out of it by other kids, Jared would slowly spread an innocent grin across his cherub-like face, allow his eyes to light up like diamonds, tilt his head slightly, and croon out the words that never failed to make everyone in the room smile.

"When I grow up," Jared would say, "I want to be a flower." Salt of the earth, that kid.

Jean and I lived near one another for most of our adult lives, so it's no surprise our children were close.

My sister and I had bonded more over the years, so our children often played together, went to school together, and, unfortunately, schemed together. More often than not, Briana and Johnathan were the ones who could be found outside the boundaries of the straight and narrow, but every now and then Jared would be gullible enough to let them draw him afoul as well.

A prime example is when Briana and Jared were taking swimming lessons together at the local YWCA. Jared was six, Briana was five, and they had both been enrolled in lessons for the previous two or three years.

Both were progressing, but neither was swimming properly yet when they got a new teacher that Briana immediately became suspicious of. Her mistrust was obvious. With just one quick glance at the new teacher, Briana's eyes narrowed to barely a squint, her little three-and-a-half-foot tall stature stiffened, and you could almost see the hairs stand up on the nape of her neck.

Their previous teacher, Mr. Ken, was a soft-spoken teenager, understanding, and too willing to negotiate—that meant Briana did exactly what Briana wanted to do.

If Briana wanted to sit on the pool deck the entire lesson, that's what she did. If she wanted to just dip her toe in the water, that's what Briana did. If she didn't want to get her hair wet, you'd better believe not a single strand became moist. Forget the fact that I was paying good money for the lessons. Briana was clearly in control of her aquatic destiny.

So, after trying to reason with her, how did I finally correct that little situation? In the only way I could.

Jared and Briana eagerly awaiting another showing of Sesame Street Live.

One day, I casually sashayed up to the registration desk and requested a different teacher, the most stern available. It wasn't that Mr. Ken was a bad instructor. On the contrary, he was quite capable. He just hadn't dealt with a Briana Nicole Hendrix before. Her strong personality needed to be matched, and Mr. Ken was just too kind to do what was going to have to be done.

Poor Jared was doing just fine with the old teacher, but since Jean and I carpooled the children, the situation meant Jared would be getting a new teacher, too.

IT'S GONNA BE TEDDY AND THE BEAR—AND THE OLD BEAR'S GONNA BE ON TOP

Miss Connie, their new swim instructor, was a whole lot different from Mr. Ken. She was an older woman in her mid-thirties, an elementary school teacher by day (so she was accustomed to head-strong children), and boy-oh-boy was she firm. Just what the doctor ordered for Briana.

On the first day, both Briana and Jared immediately noticed the change in instructors, but only Briana was bold enough to inquire about it. Jared was just happy to be there. He loved the water, so it wouldn't have mattered to him if Daffy Duck had shown up to teach. Briana, on the other hand, had become suspicious, so she didn't hesitate to ask about Mr. Ken.

Jared and Briana enjoying preschool free time

"Oh, he's teaching other children," Miss Connie politely replied.

Briana gave Miss Connie one of her signature "Huh . . . I'm not sure I believe you" looks, but she dared not say it aloud.

"So, what are we going to do today?" Briana asked after only a moment or two, obviously still trying to size up her adversary.

"Well, we're going to work on our strong kicks and bobbing underwater," Miss Connie said calmly, while pretending to be unaware of what Briana was up to.

Of course, she did know, as I had spent a great deal of time familiarizing her with Briana's personality tendencies before the lesson. Nothing like being forewarned. I couldn't send that poor woman into the situation cold. Briana may have only been five years old, but given the upper hand, she would have eaten Miss Connie alive. Before Miss Connie would have known what was happening, she would have been the one swimming laps while Briana was pacing the deck yelling that her form was all wrong. This situation called for a coordinated team approach.

Briana could be quite persistent, so I knew there would be challenges to come. But from what I'd seen, Miss Connie was up to the task. That's when I decided to leave poolside and wait in the nearby observation area where I could still see, but not hear, all that was going on.

At first, it looked like the lesson would proceed as Miss Connie had planned.

IT'S GONNA BE TEDDY AND THE BEAR—AND THE OLD BEAR'S GONNA BE ON TOP

Both Briana and Jared were in the water, holding onto the side of the pool while doing their beginning-lesson bobs.

Up, down, up, down. Breathing in their mouths on the up and out their noses on the down. Bobs were never Briana's favorite, so when I saw her colorful hair ribbons going in and out of the water, I really thought my little plan had worked.

But then I saw something unexpected. Instead of the children working on their kicks, I saw Briana climb out of the water, sit on the side of the pool, cross her little arms, and say something to her cousin to make him do the same.

Jared's gestures weren't quite as demonstrative as Briana's, and he didn't look angry. As a matter of fact, he looked afraid of Briana and unsure of what he should actually do more than anything else.

Then I glanced over at Miss Connie, and her face was even less telling. All I saw was confusion there, like a deer in headlights. She had no idea what to do next. After all I had done to try to warn Miss Connie, Briana had still gotten the jump on her.

Briana—still refusing to do those bobs

"Oh, Lord," I said to myself. "What is Briana Nicole up to now?"

Apparently, Briana had sized up Miss Connie and concluded she wasn't all that. Yes, she was an adult. Yes, she was their swim teacher. But, no, she wasn't their boss. Mr. Ken was their teacher, so HE was the boss of them.

So, when Briana decided she had done enough bobs and working on her kicks just wasn't going to happen that day, she defiantly shared her conclusion with Miss Connie and Jared.

Miss Connie, according to Briana, was not their boss, so they didn't have to do what she told them to do. And upon that revelation, Briana climbed her sassy forty-five pound frame out of the pool and told Jared he had to do the same.

Poor Jared. He complied.

IT'S GONNA BE TEDDY AND THE BEAR—AND THE OLD BEAR'S GONNA BE ON TOP

Briana had caught Miss Connie off guard, so quick action was a must. I hustled up and reached the pool deck as quickly as I possibly could. As I approached closer, I found Briana and Jared still sitting poolside and Miss Connie in the water facing them both. When she caught sight of me out of the corner of her eye, she put one finger in the air, signaling me to stop in my tracks and let her handle the situation.

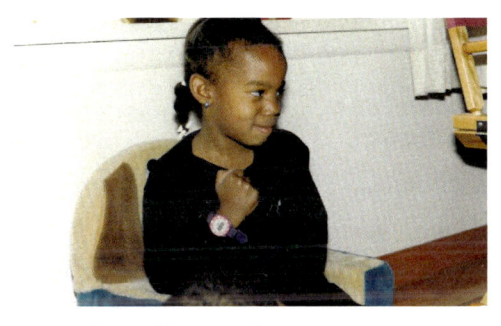

Immediately, she had my attention—and my respect.

The exchange I heard next was quite interesting.

"Briana Nicole Hendrix. What did you say?" Miss Connie asked in a voice so calm and so stern it would have made Nanny McPhee proud.

Briana showing her true colors

Ohhhh, I thought. Miss Connie started with my child's full name. That was good. Even Briana immediately saw that as a sign Miss Connie meant business, although she was still not ready to back down just yet.

"I said you're not the boss of me," Briana countered. "Mr. Ken is my boss, and he's not here. So, I don't have to do what you tell me to do."

"Oh, really? And who told you that?" Miss Connie asked.

Just for a moment, Briana hesitated. Miss Connie had asked her a question she hadn't anticipated. Briana had expected Miss Connie to let her have her way, just as Mr. Ken would have done.

But the two instructors were apples and oranges, night and day. Mr. Ken would have begged and pleaded, and "Come on, sweetied" to no avail. Briana would have sat on the pool deck until near the end of the lesson, and then jumped in the water for playtime.

It just never occurred to Briana that her outcome with Miss Connie would be any different. Poor thing. She had sized up this situation all wrong—as wrong as two left feet.

After waiting about five seconds, Miss Connie doubled down and asked the question again.

"Who told you I'm not the boss of you?"

IT'S GONNA BE TEDDY AND THE BEAR–AND THE OLD BEAR'S GONNA BE ON TOP

Briana's shifty little eyes darted back and forth until she caught a glimpse of me standing to her distant left and suddenly my name came flying out of her lying little mouth.

"My mom. My mom told me you're not the boss of us."

And with that one word, that one change in pronoun, Briana had made a power play she thought would strengthen her position. She had dragged her cousin into the fray, thinking she couldn't possibly lose because now it was two against one.

Poor Jared didn't know what to do, so he made a safe bet. He looked down into the water and never said a word.

"Oh, really?" Miss Connie retorted. "You mean your mom who's standing right there? She told you I'm not the boss of you? Well, let's ask her."

Briana looking like a storm cloud as she, Johnathan and Jared prepare for trick or treating.

Oh, this was getting good. I don't know if it was the humidity rising from the ninety-degree water, or sweat forming its telltale beads on Briana's face, but there was certainly more moisture than before rolling off her rosy round cheeks.

"Mrs. Hendrix, did you tell Briana I'm not the boss of her?" Miss Connie asked in a voice so condescending it made me proud.

"Oh, no, Miss Connie. I would never tell a five-year-old child to be so disrespectful to her adult swim teacher. Where'd you hear that?" I asked, adding to the condescension filling the room.

"Well, funny thing, Mrs. Hendrix. Briana just told me you said that, and I just couldn't believe it."

By this time, my confusion was all cleared up. Those were definitely beads of sweat rolling down Briana's face—and they were accompanied by a fearful look that said, "Oh, Lord. How am I going to get out of this?"

True to form, Briana was still quick, so she let loose another fib.

"Oh, no I didn't," she said. "I didn't say my mom told me that. I said my Boo Boo told me that."

Boo Boo with her older, more obedient grandchild—Briana

Now Boo Boo was the name all of my mom's grandchildren used for her, so now Briana was dragging her dear old granny into her mess. I recognized it as a sure sign of desperation, but Briana thought it was a stroke of genius. Miss Connie would have to believe what she said because Boo Boo wasn't there to say she didn't. And, besides, Miss Connie didn't even know who Boo Boo was. Or did she?

I'll tell you, that Miss Connie was full of tricks, and before Briana knew it, Miss Connie demonstrated who held the upper hand in their little tiff—and it wasn't the smart-alecky five-year-old.

"Ohhhhhh, I get it now," Miss Connie said slowly with a huge grin spread across her face. "You mean your Boo Boo told you I'm not the boss of you?"

Not one to rush this thing, Miss Connie waited patiently for Briana to respond.

"Yeah," Briana said boldly. "Boo Boo said only Mr. Ken was my boss at swim time—and he ain't here."

"Boy, Briana," Miss Connie continued. "That's really hard for me to believe, because the Boo Boo I teach with at Homedale Elementary School told me just today that I'd better watch out for you. She said you might not want to swim, but I should make you get your little tail in the pool because she was going to bring you back up here this weekend, and you'd better know how to do what I'm planning to teach today. As a matter of fact, she told me to call her after today's lesson to tell her how you did…and if she got a bad report, it was going to be Teddy and the Bear when you got back home."

IT'S GONNA BE TEDDY AND THE BEAR–AND THE OLD BEAR'S GONNA BE ON TOP

With that, Briana and Jared widened their eyes, opened their mouths to suck in a huge gasp of air, and straightened their little backs to attention like perfect soldiers.

"So, Briana, do me a favor?" Miss Connie requested softly. "Tell me what that means. What did Boo Boo mean when she said, 'It's gonna be Teddy and the Bear?' And, oh yeah, she also said, 'The old bear's gonna be on top.'"

Miss Connie's words took me back to my own childhood. How many times had I heard that warning? Now, even I never really knew what it meant, but it always indicated playtime was over. Mama meant business.

The original event happened before I was born, but, best I knew, the saying had come from my mother's mom, who everyone referred to as Big Mama. The story was rooted in a particularly legendary event that involved Willie L., one of Big Mama's other grandchildren, who had spent the majority of one of his teenage days fooling around the house and working Big Mama's nerves. Finally, she gave him an ominous warning by saying, "You'd better stop, Willie L., or it's gonna be Teddy and the Bear."

Willie L., probably a lot like Briana, refused to back down, and, even worse, shot back with a sarcastic, "I'll tell you what, Big Mama. If it is, I'll bet old Teddy's gonna be on top."

Boy, what did he say that for? I'm told by those in the room that all they could do was make way. Big Mama flew into Willie L. like a whirlwind, and the next thing everyone knew, his legs were flying up in the air, he was lying flat on his back, and she was straddling his body, yelling, "Who's on top, Willie L.? Who's on top?"

Willie L., clearly not in a position of strength, could only respond with a much defeated, "The old bear, Big Mama, the old bear's on top." I'm told he was a model citizen for the rest of the day.

In all of her life, my mother never laid a hand on Briana, but Briana had heard that story around the house often enough to fully comprehend the severity of her situation with Miss Connie.

So, that was it. That's all it took. Within seconds, Briana and Jared had enthusiastically jumped back into the pool and were ideal students—not just for the remainder of that lesson, but also for their next five years with Miss Connie as their swim teacher.

As a result of their obedience, they learned how to swim properly in no time, and they became two little fish with perfect form in all of the strokes. Boo

Boo's message got through loud and clear that day—neither of them wanted the old bear to be on top.

IT'S GONNA BE TEDDY AND THE BEAR–AND THE OLD BEAR'S GONNA BE ON TOP

= = = = = =
A COW NEEDS A TAIL FOR MORE THAN ONE SUMMER

If Jared, Jean's younger son, was salt of the earth, then my second born, Jerry (or Pooh as I still refer to him after twenty-two years) was—and still is—of the Himalayan Sea variety.

Unfortunately for him, having a personality akin to the purest salt known to man wasn't exactly an asset in our home. It actually put him at a distinct disadvantage when trying to survive a childhood with Briana, his shrewd, but protective older sister.

Pooh and Briana's relationship wasn't at all unusual or complicated. In fact, it was quite typical: sweet younger brother adores and worships big sister—and big sister ignores, takes advantage of, and treats little brother like dirt.

The only saving grace in it all was that Briana believed—strongly—that she was the only person who could deal harshly with her brother. If others had ever made the mistake of even thinking about looking at him sideways, she would have morphed into her mother bear mode and torn them to smithereens. Thank God no one ever did.

THE CIRCLES OF LIFE

The word "painful" doesn't come close to the emotions I felt while watching my two little acorns interact throughout their youth. I didn't like it one bit; but, truth be told, the relational inequities of it all weren't exactly foreign either.

From the moment I saw Briana hand Pooh his first slight, I felt a convictable sense of déjà vu from my own childhood. I often treated Weggie with the same nonchalance, yet she too had worshiped the ground I walked on. And, just like I had seen Weggie, Briana saw Pooh as nothing more than a little peon, more of an annoyance than anything else.

Eventually, however, my relationship with Weggie evolved into one filled with kindness and mutual respect. So, as excruciating as it was, I knew there was hope for Briana and Pooh. Until then, though, my main objective was to protect Pooh from his loving, but "sinister," sister.

The similarities between our generations reminded me of apples and trees. The former often do not fall far from the latter. And regardless of all the years Mom and I were at odds, we were now in similar positions.

For years, she had experienced my pain every time I handed Weggie a raw deal. Now, I was in the throes of a situation I had created for her all those many years ago. Remembering that was helpful, because I didn't have to reach far to discover my remedy.

Pooh sporting his first ever basketball uniform

Whenever Mom caught me mistreating Weggie, she would just fall back on her repertoire of strange sayings and utter, "Okay, Lita, you already know you're wrong, so just remember one thing. One day, Weggie is going to get fed up and dish out what you really have coming. It's like I always say, a cow needs a tail for more than one summer. Believe me, your flies will be back."

While that probably sounded like Greek to some, I knew exactly what it meant: I may have had everything I wanted in that moment, but at some point I was going to need Weggie. And because I had been unfair to her in that instant, Weggie's opportunity to pay me back was most assuredly coming. Mom believed that if there was any justice in this world at all, those flies would catch me off guard, and Weggie would refuse to be my "tail."

Of course, Mom was right. On numerous occasions throughout our childhood, Weggie was afforded the upper hand when I needed her most. Sometimes she fanned my flies; sometimes she didn't.

SURVIVING A BIG SISTER

Unfortunately, none of this did much to heal my broken heart or quell my anger whenever I caught Briana giving her affectionate and unsuspecting brother the business. Most times the poor sap never even saw it coming.

She was his big sister, the apple of his eye. He would see her through thick and thin, so whatever was his was hers. It never even occurred to Pooh that Briana's philosophy was slightly different. For her, whatever was his was hers, but whatever was hers was also hers.

As far as Briana was concerned, reciprocation was just another thirteen-letter word. But that all changed one eventful day when Briana was twelve and Pooh was eight.

See, Pooh and Briana were alike in a lot of ways. Both were incredibly athletic (although Briana played to win, and Pooh just wanted to have fun); they were both very social and had tons of friends; and they both were cool, but cerebral.

But as much as they were alike, there were also distinct differences. Pooh was an avid reader who breezed through four Harry Potter books in the summer of 2000, when he was just seven; Briana preferred kicking or dribbling a ball and abhorred turning pages. Pooh enjoyed making new creations with his thousand-plus Lego pieces; Briana could not have cared less. Pooh was pretty much a homebody who wanted his friends to sleep over at our home instead of him staying at theirs; Briana was always ready to catch the next thing departing.

Always a good sport, Pooh modeling the outfit Briana chose for him

But money management exposed the biggest difference between the two—Pooh was a real spendthrift who saved every dime. Mom often said he was so cheap, he'd skin a flea for its hide. Briana was the exact opposite. Money flowed through her hands like water. As soon as she got it, she spent it. Wonder who she got that from?

POOH'S GREAT EQUALIZER

Summer transitioned into fall in 2000, and Pooh had recently turned eight. It was the day after his big birthday bash, so we were lounging around the house, quietly discussing what he wanted to do with some of his party loot. I asked the question as more of a conversation filler, expecting full well he'd want to bank the money as usual.

But, to my surprise, Pooh had other plans. No extra savings for him, he said. He wanted to buy something special, something he'd wanted for a while, and something that would be all his: a brand new computer.

So, since I've always been a strong proponent of "If it's yours, spend it as you'd like," Pooh, Briana, and I headed to our local electronics store later that week so Pooh could check out their selection and make his purchase.

As soon as Briana entered the store, her little eyes danced like fire. She ran from the computers, to the computer games, to the gaming systems, to the CDs, to the movies. She wanted it all.

Pooh, often seen with a book in hand

Her only problem was that she couldn't afford any of it. Briana's birthday party was in October, just a mere month before Pooh's, and she had already spent every dime of her gifts. The girl was flat broke. Penniless.

But no worries, she thought. If Pooh had a computer, that pretty much meant she would have a computer. After all, what was his was hers. Right?

I knew Pooh was highly excited about his impending purchase, but from the moment we stepped foot into the store, he concealed that tidbit of information from the sales staff. His stone face didn't give one hint at what a big deal it was for him to purchase his own computer at the tender age of eight. It was all a part of his clever plan.

Instead of running around like a chicken with its head cut off, Pooh systematically and deliberately strolled through each aisle and cautiously checked the prices and features of each machine. He played the role of a seasoned shopper, looking as if it was a routine part of his normal day, and he played it well.

Pooh's purchasing technique was well executed, but it nearly fell apart when he approached the Dell Dimension desktops. He must have been overcome by the enormity of his task, but his faux pas wasn't pronounced enough for the salesperson to notice.

But as the person who knew him best, I sure did. As soon as Pooh saw the black matte casing and read the technical specs, I noticed his right eyebrow rise a bit and detected just a hint of exuberance in his voice as he grilled the salesperson with his intelligent and mature questions about the box's memory, graphics, warranty, and speed.

Once he was satisfied the machine would fit his needs, he quickly moved on to step two: negotiations. Before I knew it, the salesperson had offered Pooh a seventy-five-dollar discount for his good grades, a deep price cut on his favorite game, and we were out the door.

Pooh was super excited, I was beaming with pride, and Briana was yammering on about how convenient it was going to be for her and Pooh to no longer have to use the family computer. Poor thing. She had no idea what was ahead.

Even in that situation, Pooh was once again the unsuspecting one. He skipped out of that store excited after having just purchased his first computer, not knowing that with it came his sister's good graces. He had just fallen into his very own honey pot.

As soon as we returned home, Pooh eagerly shared with his dad every detail of the purchase, and the two of them began the unpacking and set up process. It didn't take long before two became three, as Briana weaseled her way into the mix and oohed and aahed as much as Pooh.

And then we went on about our daily lives as usual . . . well, almost as usual.

It didn't take a super sleuth to notice Briana's uncharacteristic kindness toward her brother. He gave her free use of his computer, and for the first time in his life, he experienced a benevolence from her that was normally reserved for anyone but him.

She didn't call him names like "Mr. Rabbit Teeth." She didn't trick him into doing her chores by convincing him I said

Pooh and Briana

it was his turn to do them. And she even let him tail along when she went to play with friends who had younger brothers his age.

Yep, that sister of his was the picture of best behavior. Heck, even I was shocked she knew so much about extending brotherly love. I had come to believe she didn't have it in her.

But, like they say, all good things must come to an end. Briana had used Pooh's computer like it was her own for so long, she made the fatal mistake of forgetting that it wasn't.

Unfortunately for her, Pooh was very much aware of the fact that the computer had come from his well-saved money, and that gave him the upper hand.

NOTHING LASTS FOREVER

Ironically enough, Briana's day of reckoning came through no fault of her own.

Pooh and Briana

I had played out the "Pooh bans Briana" (or "sister," as he has always referred to her) from his computer scenario in my head a thousand times before it actually happened, and every time, I imagined Briana committing some egregious act against her brother that everyone could agree was definitely unsisterly-like. But it didn't occur that way at all.

It happened only a few months after Pooh's computer purchase. He had just taken up basketball, after having found fun and success as a soccer goalie, gymnast, bowler, swimmer, and horseback rider.

Pooh's basketball team was made up of his good friends, most of whom were outstanding mini ballers. As his mom, even I had to secretly admit Pooh pretty much sucked at the game, but that didn't bother him one bit. He wasn't there to win.

Pooh was all about the socialization and just wanted to have a good time. Unlike Briana, who was a phenomenal basketball player and hated sitting on the bench, even to rest, Pooh loved riding the pine because it allowed him to chat with his friends as they exited the game for a drink or breather. His lack of skills meant he got limited minutes in each game, and that was just fine with him.

On this particular day, though, when I arrived at the gym with big Jerry,

Briana, Mom, and Dad, the coach informed us that a few guys on the team had other commitments and were unable to play. That meant the team was shorthanded, so Pooh would have to play more than his customary two to five minutes.

That in itself threw Pooh into a foul mood. He thought the coach was overstepping by expecting him to play the majority of the game.

Eventually, though, we all calmed Pooh down and told him it would be fine. His team needed him, so it was his time to step up. He grumbled a bit, but, in the end, decided to give it the old college try. He wasn't happy about it, but what other choice did he have?

Unfortunately, things went from bad to worse when he got in. Pooh's teammates actually had the audacity to pass him the ball. That rarely happened before. Not because they were selfish, but because it was clear by Pooh's facial expressions and demeanor that the ball was the last thing he wanted in the game. But this time, they had no choice. The best players were gone, the team was getting killed, and so it had to be all hands on deck.

Briana, the real baller of the house

That was hands-down the most painful sporting event either of my children has ever played in. Pooh's team was not only down the entire game, they got creamed. And just when we all thought it couldn't get any worse, the unthinkable happened.

With just seconds left to go, Pooh's teammate passed him the ball and yelled at him to shoot. In his panic that (one) he had the ball, (two) he actually had to shoot the ball, and (three) time was running out, Pooh panicked and threw the ball in the air—and it actually went in. Immediately, the crowd erupted into cheers and roars.

The ball had gone in, all right—right into the opposing team's net. Game over.

Let's just say it was a long ride home. Everyone, even Briana, tried his or her best to console Pooh. We told him it was a mistake easily made. We told him no one cared about winning or losing, that we just wanted him to have a good time. We even offered to stop for ice cream on the way. Nothing worked.

A COW NEEDS A TAIL FOR MORE THAN ONE SUMMER

When we finally arrived back home, Briana went outside to shoot hoops in the driveway and Pooh went straight to his room, which had a large window overlooking the garage and hoop.

All of a sudden, Pooh came running down the stairs looking like a storm cloud and charged straight past the grown-ups. The entire scene was so out of character for him that we called after him and followed him out the door.

What we saw shocked everyone.

Apparently, Briana had been outside demonstrating trick shots with her friend, but Pooh saw the exhibition and thought she was mocking him. Poor boy.

Normally a happy-go-lucky little sprite, it was more than Pooh could take on that day. I didn't understand everything he blurted out, and certainly don't remember it now, but we all got the gist of it. Briana's days of using his computer were over. There would be no more The Sims game. She could forget about Amazon Trail. And he didn't give a rat's patootie how she did her homework. None of that was happening ever again on his computer. She was done.

When his rampage was over, Pooh stomped right back upstairs and continued licking his wounds. The rest of us stood outside, frozen in shock.

Briana really hadn't meant him any harm. She had tried as hard as anyone to console him on the way home, but Pooh thought otherwise, and for that she had to pay.

Not surprisingly, it was Boo Boo who first emerged from her trance and broke the silence, but she didn't say a word. It was just a sound, one of the barnyard variety.

"Moooooooo," Mom said.

"What does that mean, Boo Boo?" Briana asked.

"Just ask your mom," Boo Boo said. "She knows. She heard it often enough when she was your age. You're in luck, though, because Pooh has a tender and forgiving heart. But I'd act fast, because right now you're like a cow that's missing a tail, and I do believe I hear the faint buzzing of nearby flies. And as your mom knows well, a cow needs a tail for more than one summer."

PRIDE COMES BEFORE THE FALL

The human brain has amazing memory capacity. Sometimes too incredible, as there are occasional incidents in life we'd all rather forget.

You know the kind, when you walk around all day with a booger hanging out of your nose or do that sassy strut out of the restroom with the back of your dress stuck in your panties. And then when someone finally musters up the courage to tell you, your heart just sinks at the thought of who and how many people must have seen you—and none of them had the nerve to let you know. Oh, Lord….

I must admit I've had some doozies, but my most humiliating public faux pas came as an adult, when I was attending a basketball game with Briana, my future collegiate baller.

I had been teaching at a large public university for a little more than a decade, which means I was fairly well known around the place and had been there long enough to get a little too big for my britches.

Nothing too overt or arrogant, but from time to time, I'd get a little full of myself and the haughtiness would seep through. And every time it happened, regardless of where I was, I'd hear Mom's voice as clear as a bell, chiming, "Okay, Lita, climb up on your little high horse if you want to. But be careful now, because pride comes before the fall."

Briana, a high school junior, was eager to check out the women's basketball teams of a few schools that were looking at her, so we decided to attend a Saturday afternoon game at Eastern Michigan University, the Division I school where I worked as a tenured professor of public relations.

I had watched Briana excel in athletics since she was two, and was a sports enthusiast myself, so it was an outing we were both excited about. I sometimes toyed with the idea of Briana, as well as my younger son, Jerry, pursuing a bachelor's degree at Eastern, so Briana and I both went into the game with a great deal of curiosity and elation.

As soon as we walked into the arena, we agreed it felt like a place Briana might be able to call home.

A large crowd had already assembled in Eastern's Convocation Center, a state-of-the-art, nearly 9,000-seat facility. The place wasn't full, but both the men's and women's teams were scheduled to play that day, so there were more spectators in attendance than usual.

From the moment we stepped in, I began to recognize familiar faces. I wasn't yet at the point where I would have compelled Mom to whisper a warning, but I was definitely walking taller than normal.

It felt good for Briana to see me so popular with everyone on campus, and I probably played the whole thing up more than I should have. Nothing outlandish, but I high-fived folks that day when before a simple head nod sufficed, I hugged people who normally got the standard handshake, and my more reserved professorial laugh morphed into an all-out cackle. Yep, I was most assuredly feeling myself that day.

So, with an extra spring in my step and toothy smile across my face, I yucked it up with everyone I saw all the way to our designated seats—center court, only a few rows up from the floor.

The way I paraded myself around in front of Briana that day, someone would have thought the building had been renamed Lolita's Convocation Center, and that was just fine with me.

Slowly (because when you're making an entrance, it's important that all in attendance have an opportunity to behold), I led the way as Briana and I climbed the few rows to our ideally placed seats.

I intentionally hadn't really dressed for a basketball game that day, so I sported my fitted and butter-soft black leather jacket, crisp and relaxed open white collar shirt, tight and slightly bell bottom blue jeans, and four-inch high black leather booties. Of course, my black leather bag, sparkling necklace, and large hoop earrings had been selected to match. It was the perfect ensemble—one of those outfits that had the ability to stop traffic, but didn't look like I'd worked too hard to put together. Genius!

Once seated, Briana and I were surrounded by others who I assumed were distinguished alums, or at least almost as important as I thought of myself that day.

Everyone was chatty and having a grand old time when the team's cheerleaders came around throwing T-shirts into the stands to those who were classless enough to make fools of themselves and generate the most noise.

Of course, I was not the least bit interested in making a spectacle of myself, as that would have been totally beneath someone in my elevated position.

Briana during her college basketball years

Briana, on the other hand, was an eager seventeen-year-old athlete who relished the idea of taking an authentic EMU t-shirt back to her high school friends for an impromptu session of show and tell.

The only problem was that as bold as Briana was in most situations, she could also be incredibly shy in others. And this venue was one of her "others."

It took a crafty combination of whining and flattery with phrases such as, "But Mom, you work here," and "Mom, but everyone knows you here, so they'll give you one," before I finally agreed to cop her a shirt.

Not by any means necessary, mind you. I'd do it, but on my own terms, which meant there would be no jumping up and down like a circus clown.

I made my position perfectly clear by using very specific language that started off with my nose in the clouds, and my mouth uttering in a tone so pompous it would have made Thurston Howell III of the old television show Gilligan's Island most proud, "I'm a respected full-time professor at this university, which means I have a certain reputation to maintain around here, so I'm just going to stand up and demand they give me a shirt."

Period.

Forget the fact that Mom's voice was now screaming in my ears. Forget that I had completely disregarded every lesson she and Dad had taught my sisters and me about the importance of humility. Eastern was my place, and I was going to get a shirt my way.

PRIDE COMES BEFORE THE FALL

So, when the cheerleader stood a few rows below us, I did exactly as I promised. I slowly and majestically rose to my feet, tuned out the juvenile and annoying screams of everyone around me pleading for a shirt, pointed to the cheerleader, and then returned my finger toward my body to instruct her to gently toss the shirt directly to me.

And what did she do?

Considering who I was, and who she was, she did the only thing I thought imaginable: she obliged and tossed me the shirt, of course.

You could tell it all worked out for Briana as she smiled broadly and clutched the shirt she so desperately wanted. I, on the other hand, didn't fare so well.

God does have His way of making all right with the world.

As soon as I handed Briana the shirt and bent my knees to sit, I knew the great equalizer had come to pay me a visit. Oh, and what a doozey this one would be.

See, I didn't know the thirty million dollar, 204,000-square-foot Convocation Center was filled with spring loaded seats—so when I stood up, the portion that supported my hind parts had the audacity to leap up behind me. Had I known all of that, things would have turned out much differently, but that just wasn't to be.

Instead, picture me, still in all of my "look at me 'cause I'm a big shot muckety-muck around here" high and mighty mode, nonchalantly squatting to sit back in my seat until, all of a sudden, I realized the seat was no longer there.

Imagine the unconcealed panic on my face, the widening of my eyes, the opening of my mouth, when I reached the point of no return and resigned myself to the fact that I was going down.

Two seconds later, I was the most pitiful sight ever.

With arms stretched out wide from a failed attempt to catch myself, four-inch heels reaching for the sky, and folded torso sandwiched between the seat behind me and the row in front of me, I opened my eyes to my life's greatest horror.

Everyone, and I do mean everyone, in the entire Convocation Center had their attention focused squarely on me and was laughing uncontrollably.

At first I thought it was just that ungrateful little whippersnapper of mine and the older folks seated nearby, but I then watched in horror and realized my audience was greater than I could have ever imagined.

PRIDE COMES BEFORE THE FALL

Apparently, my popularity had joined forces with the evil seating and both were biting me in the butt. One of my students, who just happened to be operating the Jumbotron that day, had seen me stand up and had the cameras focused on me the entire time. Initially, he had no way of knowing how I'd end up, but he also had no desire to point his high-resolution cameras elsewhere when things got good.

As I lay on that cold, dirty, cement floor, with no one, including Briana, breaking their laughter long enough to shimmy me out from between those rows of seats, even I had to admit I had received my just due.

My parents were not there to punish me, but the fact that I had gone from "Miss Certain Reputation" to "university-wide laughingstock" within a matter of seconds was correction enough.

All I could do was roll my head from side-to-side and whisper to myself, "Touché, Mom and Dad. Touché."

FINAL THOUGHTS

Wow – what a ride! I began writing this book so Mom would know why I love her so. I believe I accomplished that, but, as with most meaningful journeys, I also learned a few things along the way.

Being one to pride myself on knowing most everything about whatever subjects interest me, I thought I knew most every detail about Mom. Boy, was I wrong. As part of my writing process for this book, I often reached out to family and friends to help fill in the gaps of years gone by. Sometimes they gave me exactly what I was looking for, while other times they revealed events I had never known. The most surprising of which was mom's universal benevolence. Her time, her money, her expertise . . . she lovingly and generously gave it all. These people, her friends, family, former students still tell stories of how she made a positive impact on their lives. Not only have they not forgotten, many have modeled Mom throughout their own lives, and encouraged others to do the same.

As a result, I no longer reject the notion that I have turned into my mother. My children tell me I sometimes parent like her, my friends tell me I often use the same sayings as her, and it is my great hope that I have, in some way, positively touched lives like her. And it's no wonder. As Mom often said throughout my childhood when she was wary of the company I was keeping, "you never see a red bird and a black bird together." We've been in this thing side-by-side my entire life, so, yes, I am my mother's daughter!

= = = = = =

TELL US YOUR STORY...

IS YOUR FAMILY LIKE MINE?

This book contains only a fraction of mom's quirky sayings. She has nearly a hundred of them, and I'm guessing your family does as well. If so, tell us about them. Visit our website at www.LolitaCummingsCarson.com and share your sayings and stories. We'll post them on the site. And who knows, yours may even be featured in an upcoming book sequel!

Mom and Lolita, 2015

ACKNOWLEDGEMENTS

Shortly after writing my final story for this book, I began to reflect on the process, the assistance, and all who worked together to turn crazy sayings and childhood memories into a compilation of words worth reading.

It didn't take long for John Donne and his famous poem, "No Man Is An Island," to come to my remembrance. I first studied the poem decades ago in middle school as part of a class project with the best English teacher ever, Richard Plourde. Like all great educators, Mr. Plourde gave life to the piece in a way I have never forgotten. He was masterful!

The poem is brilliant and true, as its first few lines state:

> "No man is an island,
>
> Entire of itself,
>
> Every man is a piece of the continent,
>
> A part of the main."

When I think about my "main," there are some I simply must acknowledge:

Lamar Carson—my husband, best friend, chief promoter, and strong supporter.

Briana Hendrix, Jerry Hendrix II (Pooh), Daniel Carson, & Domonique Carson—my children, my loves.

Lou (Jean) Rawls and Lillian (Weggie) Cummings Pulliams—my sisters in suffering through these sayings, my friends.

Johnathan Rawls & Jared Rawls—my handsome and good-natured nephews who were once convinced "Aunt Leet" was the world's only "super genius." (How I long for those days.)

Dan Guoin—my eagle-eyed story reader, personal fitness trainer, and friend.

Wanda Harden, Gloria Coles, La'Tasha Givens, Kelsey Napier, Shannon Brown, Gabrielle Burgess-Smith, Mama Sol, Siobhan Riley —my insightful editors, my sounding boards, my friends.

Kent Gustavson—my publisher who gave me the confidence to share these stories with others. God brought us together at a time when I needed his voice. Thank you!

And finally . . .

Charles William and Mildred L. Cummings—my parents who catapulted me higher than I ever thought possible by telling me everything was within my reach. Never once did either one ever tell me there was something I could not accomplish—as long as I wasn't being lazy.

© 2015, Lolita Cummings Carson

ACKNOWLEDGEMENTS

TESTIMONIALS

These stories recall what might be considered a simpler time in American life, but they are foremost a testament to the enduring family values that helped to keep Black families anchored and secure in a world where they were sometimes not respected. Cummings Carson's humorous look at growing up in Flint in the '70s is punctuated by her mother's homespun proverbs, including the title, A Cow Needs A Tail For More Than One Summer. Not surprising that the sage advice embodied in these colorful sayings finds its way to the next generation of Cummings children. Readers will find themselves smiling in recognition, remembering similar advice given in their own families, and thanking Lolita for putting pen to paper.

Gloria Coles

Retired Director, Flint Public Library

Very necessary, A Cow Needs A Tail For More Than One Summer: Life Lessons from Mom takes the reader on a journey of transformation. Growth, experience, wisdom . . . depending on the reader, there are so many different ways to learn from this collection. Several perspectives shared. What an inspiring collection of literature, of truth: a child's truth, the truth of a preteen, the truth of a teen-turned-adult-turned-mother, all experienced through one set of eyes. Literature celebrating maturation and applied wisdom for the common good.

Mama Sol

Lyricist, poet, motivational speaker & front woman of MAMA SOL & THA N.U.T.S.

Momma knows best! Full of humor and wit, Carson takes us on a coming-of-age journey based on wise old sayings passed down from her mother. Her sage advice still resonates in the life of this contemporary daughter, sister, wife, and mother. So "If I tell you a hen dips snuff, you look under the wing." You won't be disappointed.

Wanda Harden

Public Relations Coordinator, Flint Public Library (MI)

A Cow Needs A Tail For More Than One Summer: Life Lessons from Mom is an amazing read! It's a tale of great parenting, a strong-willed child, and principles that stand the test of time. The main character, Lolita, now a mother herself, takes you on a journey as she learns life lessons...many of them the hard way.

Using Southern sayings from a time gone by, Lolita's mother attempts to instill in her children values and principles that can't be bought, only taught by a wise soul.

The compilation of ten short stories is a wonderful tribute to parents who plant a daily seed of wisdom in their children, hoping it sprouts a well-rounded, kind person.

Lolita was able to pass down these teachings to her own children. Both are now adults having a positive impact on society, ultimately proving the Bible verse, "If you train a child in the way he should go, when he is old he will not depart . . . ." (Proverbs 22:6 King James Version KJV)

La'Tasha Givens

11 Alive News Reporter, Atlanta, GA

ABOUT THE AUTHOR

LOLITA CUMMINGS CARSON, APR

Lolita Cummings Carson, author of "A Cow Needs a Tail For More Than One Summer: Life Lessons From Mom," has proven her expertise in areas far beyond cows, tails and parenting.

Cummings Carson specializes in public relations and has worked as a full professor at Eastern Michigan University in Ypsilanti, Mich., for more than two decades. Before entering academia, she worked as a successful public relations professional for numerous nonprofit organizations and a fortune 500 corporation for nearly 10 years. She continues to consult with nonprofit organizations and businesses whose mission and work speaks to her heart, specializing in corporate social responsibility, strategic planning, crisis communication, promotions, marketing, grant writing and professional writing.

When asked what aspect of her personality has most helped her succeed, Cummings Carson was direct and decisive.

"Focus and integrity," she said. "I know what I am doing five minutes from now, five days from now, five years from now. I always have a plan – and that plan is always centered in truth, honesty and transparency."

Cummings Carson, an accredited member of the Public Relations Society of America (PRSA), earned a bachelor's degree in Communications from Western Michigan University and a master's degree in Communications from Eastern Michigan University. She is a sought after thought leader who connects serious social issues with the hilarious sayings in her book. Such topics cross all generations and audiences -- and include corporate social responsibility, effective parenting, financial literacy, healthy and peaceful living, personal responsibility and accountability, thoughtful decision-making, learning from mistakes, and more!

Contact Lolita Cummings Carson, APR at:

Email: Lcummin2@emich.edu • **Web address:** LolitaCummingsCarson.com

Instagram: @LolitaCCarson • **Facebook:** facebook.com/lolita.ccarson

Twitter: @LolitaCCarson • **LinkedIn:** linkedin.com/in/lolitaccarson

ABOUT THE AUTHOR

Made in the USA
San Bernardino, CA
29 January 2016